Contents

These are Vegetarian Times

Good for you. You're eating better and taking care of yourself. Whether you are a vegetarian in the strictest sense of the word or are simply choosing more meatless meals, we know you're busy and you want good food too. These recipes have been carefully chosen with your needs in mind.

You are about to be dazzled with flavor and delighted with results. These easy-to-follow recipes yield some of my personal favorites, from Indian Pudding to Black Bean Quesadillas. I know you'll love the old favorites, like Vegetable Lasagna and Cream of Mushroom Soup (without the cream), but I hope you'll also try the unfamiliar ones, such as Mandarin Salad with Tempeh, and Jolof Rice. I promise some of these recipes will become your kitchen standbys—and family favorites—in no time.

Have fun! And here's to your health!

Toni Apgar

Toni Apgar
Editorial Director, *Vegetarian Times*

Special thanks to recipe developers: Nava Atlas, Ann Burckhardt, Mary Carroll, Susan Jane Cheney, Bryanna Clark Grogan, Yamuna Devi, Jeannine Johnson Perriseau, Lillian Kayte, Bharti Kirchner, Phyllis Kohn, Laura Leininger, Miyoko Nishimoto, Diana Shaw Clark, Jennifer Smith Austin, Jay Solomon and Charlie Trotter, and to Vegetarian Times Food Editor Carol Wiley Lorente.

Photographers: Cy DeCosse Incorporated, McCormick and Nelson Inc., Alison Miksch, Diana O. Rasche and Kevin Smith.

Editorial Coordinator: Janet Villano

Creative Director	Cherie B. Lee
Art Director	Will Lotzow
Electronic Production	Lori Schneider
Traffic Manager	Susan Erickson
Illustration	Bill Nelson
Photographer	Chuck Nields
Food Stylists	Abby Wyckoff
	Nancy J. Johnson
Prop Stylist	Michelle Joy
Production Manager	Laurie Gilbert

on the cover: Vegetable Lasagna, see page 58
Printed in U.S.A.

Vegetarian Basics

The term vegetarian may seem simple enough to understand. Yet there are as many degrees and varieties of vegetarianism as there are reasons for adopting a vegetarian lifestyle.

Most people become interested in vegetarianism when they make the connection between nutrition and disease prevention. They begin by cutting out foods that were once considered essential and adding a variety of plant-based foods. The first item to be eliminated from the diet is usually red meat or beef, followed by pork, poultry and fish. People who decrease their intake of some or all of these foods often consider themselves vegetarians or semi-vegetarians.

Those people who completely eliminate beef, pork, poultry and fish from their diets are what most people consider true vegetarians. Another term for this type of eater is ovo-lacto vegetarian. This simply means a vegetarian who consumes eggs and dairy products such as milk and cheese. Similarly, a lacto-vegetarian is one who consumes dairy products, but no eggs.

The purest form of vegetarianism is veganism. Unlike ovo-lacto vegetarians, vegans have eliminated all animal products from their diets. In addition to the elimination of eggs and dairy products, many vegans also avoid consuming animal byproducts such as honey.

Although all of the recipes contained in this book are vegetarian (contain no beef, pork, poultry or fish), they are further classified as either vegan, lacto or ovo-lacto, as indicated at the end of each recipe.

Nutritional information is also provided that lists the number of calories, and the amount of protein, fat, carbohydrates, cholesterol, sodium and fiber per serving. When a choice of ingredients is given, the breakdown reflects the first ingredient listed. When there is a range of servings, the breakdown reflects the first number listed. See page 96 for further explanation of these figures.

The Recipe Index on pages 94 and 95 offers an easy-to-read breakdown of each recipe's classification. It also indicates which recipes are considered to be low-fat, containing less than 10 grams of fat per serving.

Many of the recipes included in this book offer ingredient substitutions, such as soymilk in place of regular dairy milk. These substitutions may turn a lacto recipe into a vegan recipe or an ovo-lacto recipe into a lacto recipe. When this occurs, both classifications are listed.

The Glossary on page 92 offers definitions and explanations of uncommon ingredients, with which you may not be familiar.

20 Reasons to Be a Vegetarian

If you need some answers to the endless queries of well-meaning friends—
this list should keep you happy, healthy, veg and proud of it.

1. It's Heart-Smart—Countless research studies from as far back as the 1970s show that heart disease can be prevented with a low-fat vegetarian diet. A very strict low-fat vegetarian diet can even reverse heart disease.

2. It Puts a Dent in Diabetes—Diabetes is rare among Africans, Asians and Polynesians who eat foods that are primarily starches, vegetables and fruits. However, when these people learn to eat the things offered by the rich Western diet, diabetes and complications of atherosclerosis flourish in all of them. So find your tropical inner child: Return to the fruit, vegetable and whole grain-based diet you (and your blood sugar) will appreciate.

3. High Blood Pressure Takes a Hiatus—A study in the medical journal *The Lancet* found that polyunsaturated vegetable fats tend to lower blood pressure, while animal fats raise it. Best bet—avoid the animals altogether and keep total fat to a minimum. Walk that walk, swim that swim, or whack that tennis ball when life's stresses become overwhelming. Breathe deeply, eat your greens, and you may be off those multiple medications in no time.

4. It's Good for Your Pocketbook—It's far cheaper to buy a sack of potatoes or a bunch of carrots than ground sirloin. Vegetable kebobs cost a fraction of meat or fish kebobs. However, if you eat only processed, prepared foods, being veg may not seem like a bargain. Buy your grains in bulk, buy seasonal produce, and make as much as you can yourself. And if you want to splurge on extra-juicy organic blackberries or some one-of-a-kind exotic vegetables, do it with a clear conscience: You're saving on medical bills, useless diet powders and maybe even medication.

5. Being Veg Is Green and Clean—It takes far less land, water and money to grow grain than it takes to produce beef. Fact: 64 percent of American agricultural land is used to grow livestock feed. Fact: 60 million metric tons of methane gas (that's the one that is contributing to global warming) is belched by U.S. cattle annually. The current emphasis on high-volume farm production is also taking a bite out of your taxes, with $10 billion in federal funds going to price supports for beef and veal, and $13 billion for milk price supports.

6. It's Energy-Efficient—We all know that high-carb meatless pasta is the meal of choice for runners, delivering slow, sustained energy without excess fat and calories. But eating low on the food chain can save the earth some energy, too. To get one calorie of protein from soybeans, 2 calories of fossil fuel are expended; however, to get one calorie of protein from beef, a whopping 78 calories of fossil fuel must be used.

7. Water, Water Isn't Everywhere—Drink in these facts during the next drought: 50 percent of U.S. water is used for some phase of livestock production. It takes 2,500 gallons of water to produce one pound of meat, but only 25 gallons to produce one pound of wheat.

8. You Can Help Creatures Great and Small—Many who turn to vegetarianism for health reasons soon discover a heightened awareness of animal welfare and environmental issues. Compassion for all beings is a natural part of vegetarianism; by not eating meat, you're standing up to the practice of cruel factory farming. By refusing to eat meat, you can save thousands of animals from miserable conditions.

9. It Adds Variety and Spice to Life—We guarantee you'll become the most sought-after dinner host in your social set. With no "hunk-of-meat-in-the-middle-of-the plate" constraints, you're free to experiment with new recipes, exotic produce, and the cuisines of the globe. Recent issues of *Vegetarian Times* have highlighted Peruvian, Thai and Indonesian fare. Try a few great new dishes, and watch the raves pour in.

10. You'll Be on the Fast Track—Pasta power is in, slabs o' steak are out. As anyone from bodybuilders to Ironman triathletes will tell you, a vegetarian diet is the way to go for beautiful muscles, great strength and endless endurance. Contrary to the belief that protein builds muscles, it's actually the continuous stressing and development of the muscles that gets you in shape. And if anyone asks where you get your protein, smile, finish your fifth Nautilus set and tell them that the Recommended Dietary Allowance for protein is 63 grams for men, and 50 for women; most vegetarians exceed that by at least 15 grams.

11. **Grain Goes Farther**—Grains and soybeans that are now fed to U.S. livestock could feed 1.3 billion people, according to the North American Vegetarian Society.

12. **Cleaning's a Breeze**—No more of those greasy, hard-to-clean barbecue grills or, to quote vegetarian chef Annie Somerville, "duck legs sticking up out of the stock and carcasses everywhere." And no more worrying about salmonella from raw chicken lurking around your cutting board. You can invite your parents to dinner and impress them with your clean kitchen.

13. **You're in Good Company**—Join the ranks of an impressive group of vegetarians throughout history, traversing the fields of science, literature and music. Prominent thinkers, movers and shakers who took the veg road include George Bernard Shaw, Mahatma Gandhi, Albert Einstein, Paul McCartney and Hank Aaron, to name only a few.

14. **You Get a Nutritional Boost**—The more fruits, vegetables and grains you eat, the more nutritional "bang" you get from your food. On a varied veg diet, it's easy to get the iron and calcium you need without a lot of added fat. Three-fourths of a cup of spinach, for instance, contains a half to a third of recommended daily intake of iron, depending on gender, with only .15 grams of fat. Calorie for calorie, spinach has 14 times the iron of sirloin steak.

15. **You Can Be the Focus of Dinner Conversation**—Who needs celebrity scandals when you've got a veggie burger? People will ask about your vegetarianism; a few might be defensive or aggressive, but most will be genuinely curious. Share your reasons and recipes with a receptive audience, and clear up those common misconceptions about protein intake.

16. **You Can Finally Solve the Mystery of Tofu**—No more wondering what those soft white blocks are really for. You may amaze yourself (and your skeptical friends) when you find yourself actively seeking new ways to add these flavor-absorbing, nutrient-packed soyfoods to your diet. We don't know why they've gotten a bad rap, when they can be turned into everything from a Tempeh Reuben to a Chocolate Mousse Pie.

17. **It Will Increase Your Nutrition Knowledge**—As a vegetarian, you'll find yourself gradually absorbing all kinds of nutritional information. It happens to the best of us: First you're eating the broccoli, then you're reading about it, and before long, you know how rich it is in calcium, and how that calcium helps keep your bones from thinning. Soon you'll be able to talk carbohydrates, vitamins and protein with the best of them.

18. **You'll Have Something in Common with Generation X**—You may not be into Pearl Jam, and baggy pants don't fit into your wardrobe, but you and all of the teens in your life can share an interest in vegetarianism. More and more teens are turning to (and sticking to) a meatless diet. It's a great way to open a dialogue about compassion, responsibilities and— a subject dear to most teens' hearts—food!

19. **It Nourishes Your Body and Mind**—As a vegetarian, you'll find yourself thinking about the effects of your food and lifestyle choices on the environment, on animals and on yourself. Being a vegetarian is more than just the food on your plate; even as you enjoy the food, the wider-reaching benefits may also nourish you on an intellectual or spiritual level.

20. **It's a Way of Life**—Currently 12.4 million Americans call themselves vegetarians. You've read about it in the newspapers, seen it on your grocery shelves and heard about it on the talk shows. It makes sense, it's fun, and now you're a part of it. Vegetarianism is more than a trend—it's a lifestyle that's here to stay.

Appetizers
& Snacks

Asparagus Guacamole, see page 8

Asparagus Guacamole

1 lb. fresh asparagus spears, cut into 1-inch lengths (2 cups)

$3/4$ cup water

2 Tbs. plain nonfat or low-fat yogurt

1 Tbs. lemon juice

1 medium tomato, seeded and chopped (1 cup)

2 Tbs. sliced green onion

1 tsp. ground cumin

1 clove garlic, minced

$1/2$ tsp. dried oregano leaves

$1/4$ tsp. salt

$1/4$ tsp. cayenne

Combine asparagus and water in a 2-quart saucepan. Bring to a boil over medium-high heat. Cover and reduce heat to medium-low. Simmer 8 to 10 minutes, or until asparagus is tender. Rinse with cold water; drain. Blot asparagus with paper towel to remove excess moisture.

Combine asparagus, yogurt and lemon juice in a food processor or blender. Process until smooth. In a medium mixing bowl, combine asparagus mixture and remaining ingredients. Chill, if desired. Serve with raw vegetables or tortilla chips. Makes 12 servings.

PER SERVING: 12 CAL.; 1G PROT.; <1G FAT; 2G CARB.; <1MG CHOL.; 51MG SOD.; 1G FIBER. LACTO

MICROWAVE TIP: Reduce water to 2 tablespoons. In a 2-quart casserole, combine asparagus and water. Cover and microwave on high power 6 to 8 minutes, or until asparagus is tender, stirring once. Continue as directed.

Steamed Vegetable Platter with Curried Hummus Dip

Dip:
19-oz. can garbanzo beans, rinsed
  and drained
2 Tbs. snipped fresh parsley
1 to 2 Tbs. lemon juice
1 Tbs. olive oil
1 Tbs. sesame oil
2 tsp. soy sauce
1 clove garlic, minced

$^{1}/_{4}$ tsp. freshly ground pepper
$^{1}/_{4}$ tsp. curry powder

Platter:
5 oz. baby zucchini (about 12)
10 cups water
2 cups cauliflower florets
5 oz. baby carrots (1 cup)

Hummus: In a food processor or blender, combine all ingredients. Process until smooth, scraping sides of bowl periodically. Transfer hummus to small serving bowl; place in center of large serving platter. Set aside.

Platter: Starting $^{3}/_{4}$ inch from stem end of each zucchini, cut $^{1}/_{4}$-inch strips, leaving strips attached at end. In a 4-quart saucepan, bring water to a boil over high heat. Immerse zucchini in water $1^{1}/_{2}$ to 2 minutes, or until color brightens and zucchini are crisp-tender. Remove with slotted spoon and plunge immediately into ice water; drain. Repeat procedure with cauliflower and carrots.

Arrange zucchini around hummus on platter, pressing zucchini lightly to fan. Arrange cauliflower and carrots around zucchini. Makes 4 to 6 servings.

PER SERVING: 256 CAL.; 9G PROT.; 9G FAT; 38G CARB.; 0 CHOL.; 587MG SOD.; 9G FIBER.
VEGAN

Cinnamon Chips with Crenshaw Salsa

1/4 cup plus 2 Tbs. sugar, divided
2 tsp. cornstarch
1 tsp. grated lemon peel
1/2 cup water
1 Tbs. lemon juice

3 cups finely chopped
    Crenshaw melon
1 tsp. ground cinnamon
6 8-inch flour tortillas
Red cinnamon candies (optional)

In a 1-quart casserole, combine 1/4 cup sugar, cornstarch and lemon peel. Blend in water and juice. Cook, stirring constantly, over medium heat 3 1/2 to 7 minutes, or until mixture is thickened and translucent. In a medium mixing bowl, combine lemon mixture and melon. Cover and chill.

Preheat oven to 375 degrees. In a large plastic food-storage bag or paper bag, combine remaining 2 tablespoons sugar and cinnamon; set aside. Spray both sides of tortillas with vegetable cooking spray; cut each into 6 wedges. Place wedges in bag. Secure bag and shake to coat.

Arrange 12 wedges in a single layer on baking sheet. Bake 5 to 8 minutes, or until light golden brown. Repeat with remaining tortilla wedges. Cool completely. Garnish salsa with cinnamon candies, if desired, and serve. Makes 6 servings.

PER SERVING: 106 CAL.; 1G PROT.; 1G FAT; 23G CARB.; 0MG CHOL.; 42MG SOD.; 1G FIBER.
VEGAN

Cinnamon Chips with Crenshaw Salsa

Crispy Baked Egg Rolls

$^1/_4$ cup water
1 cup diced onion
1 Tbs. minced ginger root
4 cloves garlic, minced
2 cups diced celery
$^1/_2$ cup diced fresh shiitake
    mushrooms
$^1/_2$ cup diced domestic white
    mushrooms

3 cups diced green cabbage
1 cup diced bamboo shoots
1 cup diced water chestnuts
2 Tbs. low-sodium soy sauce
1 Tbs. rice wine or mirin
1 Tbs. honey
24 egg roll wrappers
2 Tbs. dark sesame oil, warmed

Preheat oven to 400 degrees. Heat water in a wok until simmering. Stir-fry onion, ginger and garlic until onion is soft but not browned, about 5 minutes. Add celery, shiitake and white mushrooms, cabbage, bamboo shoots and water chestnuts; stir-fry until vegetables soften, about 5 to 8 minutes. Remove from heat. Add soy sauce, rice wine or mirin, and honey; toss well. Place mixture in colander over a bowl; let stand 10 minutes to drain off excess moisture.

Dry counter or tabletop for egg roll wrapping. Have a small bowl of water ready. Stack egg roll wrappers with one corner pointing away from you. Spoon $^1/_4$ cup drained filling into center of each wrapper. Lightly brush edges of wrapper with water.

Fold side corners to center, covering filling. Next bring bottom corner to center; over and then under filling and continue to roll wrapper into a cylinder, sealing top corner by moistening slightly with water and pressing down.

Lightly spray two nonstick baking sheets with vegetable cooking spray. Place egg rolls seam side down on sheets. (Do not crowd). Lightly brush with sesame oil. Bake 15 to 20 minutes in center of oven, until golden and crispy, turning once. Serve immediately. Makes 24 egg rolls.

PER EGG ROLL: 80 CAL.; 3G PROT.; 1G FAT; 14G CARB.; 0 CHOL.; 66MG SOD.; 1G FIBER.
OVO-LACTO

TIP: Low-fat stir-fries are easily created by heating a liquid other than oil (such as cooking sherry, rice wine or vegetable broth) until it bubbles. Vegetables will take a bit longer to soften than if you used oil. Don't worry if you don't have a wok; a large, nonstick skillet makes a great stir-frying tool.

Natural Peanut Butter Fruit Dip

8-oz. package light cream cheese, softened
1/2 cup packed brown sugar
1/2 cup all natural creamy peanut butter
1/2 cup chopped unsalted dry-roasted peanuts
4 cups water
1/4 cup lemon juice
2 medium green apples, cored and sliced
1 medium red apple, cored and sliced
2 cups hulled whole strawberries
7 celery sticks, tops included

In a small mixing bowl, combine cream cheese, brown sugar, peanut butter and peanuts; mix well. Transfer dip to serving bowl; set aside.

In a large mixing bowl, combine water and juice. Immerse apple slices in water to prevent discoloring; drain. Arrange dip, apple slices, strawberries and celery on serving platter. Garnish dip with additional chopped peanuts, if desired. Makes 16 servings.

PER SERVING: 146 CAL.; 5G PROT.; 9G FAT; 14G CARB.; 5MG CHOL.; 99MG SOD.; 2G FIBER.
LACTO

Caponata

1/4 cup plus 1 Tbs. olive oil, divided
1 medium eggplant (1 lb.), cut into 3/4-inch cubes
1 clove garlic, minced
1 tsp. salt
1/2 cup chopped onion
1/3 cup sliced celery
16-oz. can Roma tomatoes, drained and diced
1/3 cup halved pitted medium black olives
1/4 cup red wine vinegar
1 Tbs. capers, drained
1 Tbs. snipped fresh oregano leaves
1/4 tsp. freshly ground pepper
1/4 cup toasted pine nuts
Toasted Italian or French bread slices
2 Tbs. margarine or butter
1/4 cup Parmesan cheese

In a 12-inch nonstick skillet, heat 1/4 cup oil over medium heat. Add eggplant, garlic and salt; cook 5 to 7 minutes, or until eggplant is golden brown, stirring occasionally. Remove from heat; set aside.

In a 2-quart casserole, combine remaining oil, onion and celery. Microwave on high power 5 to 7 minutes, or until onion is tender, stirring once. Stir in tomatoes, olives, vinegar, capers, oregano and pepper. Cover. Microwave on high power 4 to 6 minutes, or until mixture is hot and flavors are blended, stirring once.

Stir in eggplant mixture and pine nuts. Cool slightly. Cover and chill overnight, stirring occasionally. Serve on slices of toasted bread that have been lightly buttered and sprinkled with Parmesan cheese. Makes 16 servings.

PER SERVING: 168 CAL.; 4G PROT.; 9G FAT; 19G CARB.; 3MG CHOL.; 521MG SOD.; 2G FIBER.
LACTO

Seasoned Chips with Lone Star 'Caviar'

Seasoned Chips with Lone Star 'Caviar'

2 medium tomatoes, seeded and chopped (2 cups)

15-oz. can black-eyed peas, rinsed and drained

1 medium green bell pepper, chopped ($1^1/3$ cups)

$1/2$ cup sliced green onions

$1/2$ cup snipped fresh cilantro leaves

2 Tbs. lemon juice

2 serrano peppers, seeded and finely chopped

1 to 2 jalapeño peppers, seeded and finely chopped

2 cloves garlic, minced

$2^1/4$ tsp. ground cumin, divided

$1/2$ tsp. salt

2 tsp. chili powder

1 tsp. garlic powder

16 6-inch whole wheat flour tortillas

'Caviar': Combine tomatoes, peas, bell pepper, onions, cilantro, lemon juice, serrano peppers, jalapeño peppers, garlic, $1/4$ teaspoon cumin and salt in a medium mixing bowl. Cover with plastic wrap. Chill at least 4 hours to blend flavors, stirring occasionally.

Chips: Preheat oven to 375 degrees. In a large plastic food-storage bag or paper bag, combine remaining 2 teaspoons cumin, chili powder and garlic powder; set aside. Spray both sides of each tortilla with vegetable cooking spray; cut each into 8 wedges. Place wedges in bag. Secure bag and shake to coat.

Arrange 32 wedges in a single layer on a baking sheet. Bake 7 to 9 minutes, or until light golden brown. Repeat with remaining tortilla wedges. Cool completely. Serve with 'Caviar.' Makes 16 servings.

PER SERVING: 111 CAL.; 4G PROT.; 1G FAT; 28G CARB.; 0 CHOL.; 304MG SOD.; 2G FIBER.
VEGAN

MICROWAVE TIP: Arrange 16 seasoned wedges in single layer on a paper towel-lined plate. Microwave on high power 4 to 5 minutes or until crisp, rotating plate once. Loosen chips from paper towel immediately. Repeat with remaining tortilla wedges. Continue as directed.

Soups
& Stews

Corn and Potato Chowder, see page 18

Corn and Potato Chowder

1 tsp. safflower oil
2 tsp. dry sherry or water
1 1/2 cups finely chopped onion
1 cup thinly sliced carrot
2 stalks celery with leaves, thinly
    sliced
1 bay leaf

2 cups cubed red potatoes
1 cup vegetable stock
1 cup skim milk
1 cup fresh or frozen corn kernels
Cayenne pepper to taste
Nonfat plain yogurt for garnish
    (optional)

In a large, heavy saucepan, heat oil, and sherry or water until bubbling. Add onion and sauté 5 minutes, stirring frequently to prevent browning. (If mixture appears dry, add 1 to 2 tablespoons water.) Add carrot, celery, bay leaf, potatoes and stock. Cover pan, bring to a boil and cook over medium heat 10 to 15 minutes, or until potato is tender. Add milk and corn; simmer 3 minutes, or until corn is tender. Discard bay leaf.

In a food processor or blender, process 1 cup soup until smooth, then return to pan. Season with cayenne. If desired, garnish with a dollop of nonfat yogurt. Makes 4 servings.

PER SERVING: 196 CAL.; 5G PROT.; 1G FAT; 39G CARB.; 1MG CHOL.; 83MG SOD.; 7G FIBER.
LACTO

Cream of Mushroom Soup

10½ oz. silken tofu
1 cup water
1 medium onion, chopped
5 cloves garlic, pressed or minced
1 Tbs. soy margarine or butter
8 oz. mushrooms, thickly sliced

1 tsp. thyme
½ cup sherry or other dry red wine
1 tsp. low-sodium soy sauce
Pinch cayenne pepper
Salt to taste

Combine tofu and ¼ cup water in a food processor or blender. Process about 2 minutes, or until smooth. Add remaining ¾ cup water; process until blended.

In a large skillet, sauté onion and garlic in margarine or butter just until onion is translucent, about 5 minutes. Add mushrooms and thyme; sauté 5 minutes more. Add sherry or red wine; simmer 5 minutes.

Add a ladle of the cooking liquid to tofu-water mixture; process a few seconds until smooth. Pour tofu mixture into skillet with mushroom mixture and add soy sauce and cayenne; stir. Salt to taste. Simmer until mushrooms are wilted and flavors have melded. Makes 6 servings.

Variation: You may substitute 5 teaspoons plum sauce as a non-alcoholic alternative to the wine; however, this will add a slight sweetness to the soup.

PER SERVING: 99 CAL.; 4G PROT.; 3G FAT; 8G CARB.; 5MG CHOL.; 64MG SOD.; 1G FIBER.
VEGAN/LACTO

TIP: You can use this soup as an ingredient just as easily as you'd use the canned variety: Just dice the mushrooms, and thin the soup with a little more water—¼ to ½ cup. Or, using the reduced amount of water, you can cook the soup until the mushrooms are very soft, and purée all of the ingredients before adding it to another recipe.

Thinned down a bit, this soup makes a good stroganoff-type sauce for grains or pasta, or as an ingredient in your favorite vegetarian loaf or burger mixture.

Lemon Broth with Eggplant Wontons

Lemon Broth with Eggplant Wontons

Wontons:

1 cup finely diced red bell pepper

$1^{1}/_{2}$ lbs. eggplant (2 medium), diced

2 hot chili peppers, any variety

1 tsp. grated ginger root

3 Tbs. minced cilantro

$^{1}/_{2}$ Tbs. toasted sesame seeds

1 tsp. toasted sesame oil

Salt and pepper to taste

48 wonton wrappers

Broth:

6 cups vegetable broth

1 cup water

$1^{1}/_{2}$ Tbs. lemon juice

$^{1}/_{2}$ Tbs. grated lemon zest

1 cup julienned snow peas or 2 cups spinach chiffonade (rolled and cut into strips)

1 Tbs. julienned cilantro leaves

1 green chili pepper, any variety, seeded and thinly sliced crosswise

A few drops infused oil or sesame oil (optional)

Wontons: Steam bell pepper and eggplant until tender, about 6 to 8 minutes. Transfer to a bowl, cool slightly and coarsely mash with a fork. Add all remaining ingredients except wonton wrappers; mix well. To make wontons, brush wrapper surface with water. Place about 2 teaspoons eggplant filling in center of wrapper. Fold top edge over filling to meet bottom edge. Press edges to seal. Continue until you've used all filling and wrappers.

Broth: In a large soup pot, bring broth, water, juice and zest to a boil. Boil about 3 minutes. Stir in peas or spinach and turn off heat.

In a separate pot, bring 1 quart water to a boil. Add wontons and cook a few at a time until they float to the surface, about 3 minutes.

To serve: Place 8 wontons and about 1 cup lemon broth in a shallow soup bowl. Garnish with cilantro, chili pepper and infused oil or sesame oil, if desired. Makes 6 servings.

Variation: For a more substantial meal, add 4 oz. wheat noodles to broth and simmer 3 minutes before adding cooked wontons.

PER SERVING: 294 CAL.; 11G PROT.; 3G FAT; 55G CARB.; 0 CHOL.; 278MG SOD.; 5G FIBER. OVO-LACTO

Cantaloupe Soup

Cantaloupe Soup

1 medium-sized cantaloupe
1 cup orange juice
2 tsp. fresh lime juice
1 cup plain nonfat yogurt

Fresh mint leaves cut into strips
(optional)
Slivers of melon for garnish

Quarter melon. Remove and discard seeds, and cut fruit from rind. Dice fruit and place in a food processor or blender. Add orange and lime juices; pureé.

Place yogurt in a glass mixing bowl and beat with a whisk until light and smooth. Whisk in melon mixture.

Cover bowl and refrigerate at least 3 hours, until chilled through and flavors have melded. Serve cold, sprinkled with fresh mint leaves and melon slivers if desired. Makes 4 servings.

PER SERVING: 110 CAL.; 5G PROT.; <1G FAT; 21G CARB.; 1MG CHOL.; 61MG SOD.; 1G FIBER.
LACTO

Anasazi Bean Soup

1 cup dry anasazi beans, picked
over and rinsed
Vegetable stock or water
1 medium onion, chopped
2 large cloves garlic, pressed or
minced
$1/4$ tsp. ground coriander

$1/2$ tsp. ground cumin
1 jalapeño or other pepper,
finely chopped
Salt to taste
Minced green onions and/or
cilantro leaves for garnish

Cover beans with water and soak overnight, allowing extra water for expansion. Drain, reserving soaking water. Measure soaking water and add stock or water to equal 6 cups. Pour into pot.

Add remaining ingredients except salt, green onion and cilantro, and bring to a boil. Cover, reduce heat and cook at a low simmer $1\frac{1}{2}$ to 2 hours, or until beans are tender. Season with salt to taste and serve hot, garnished with green onion and/or cilantro. Makes 4 servings.

PER SERVING: 183 CAL.; 10G PROT.; <1G FAT; 32G CARB.; 0 CHOL.; 422MG SOD., 6G FIBER.
VEGAN

Ratatouille and Bean Stew

1 medium onion, sliced and
    separated into rings
1 Tbs. olive oil
1 medium eggplant (about 1 lb.), cut
    into $1/2$-inch cubes
28-oz. can plum tomatoes, drained
    and diced
2 cups sliced zucchini

1 medium green bell pepper,
    cut into strips
2 tsp. dried parsley flakes
1 to 2 tsp. dried oregano leaves
$1/2$ tsp. salt
$1/2$ tsp. sugar
15-oz. can chili beans in sauce

In a 4-quart saucepan, combine onion and oil. Cook over medium heat 5 to 7 minutes, or until onion is tender, stirring occasionally.

Add all remaining ingredients except beans. Cover and cook over low heat 25 to 30 minutes, or until eggplant is tender and translucent, stirring occasionally. Add beans. Mix well and cook, uncovered, 5 to 7 minutes, or until hot, stirring occasionally. Makes 6 servings.

PER SERVING: 167 CAL.; 8G PROT.; 4G FAT; 25G CARB.; 0 CHOL.; 543MG SOD.; 11G FIBER.
VEGAN

Indonesian Vegetable Soup

$1^{1}/2$ cups finely shredded red
    cabbage
1 cup sliced green beans ($1/2$-inch
    lengths)
$1/2$ cup diagonally sliced carrots
$1/2$ cup chopped onion
1 Tbs. vegetable oil

$14^{1}/2$-oz. can vegetable broth
1 cup water
1 cup uncooked instant white rice
$1/2$ cup raisins
1 tsp. grated ginger root
$1/2$ tsp. turmeric
$1/4$ tsp. ground cinnamon

In a 12-inch nonstick skillet, combine cabbage, beans, carrots, onion and oil. Cook over medium heat, stirring frequently, 5 to 8 minutes, or until beans are crisp-tender. Add remaining ingredients; mix well.

Bring mixture to a boil over high heat. Reduce heat to low. Cover and simmer 8 to 10 minutes, or until vegetables are tender and flavors are blended, stirring occasionally. Makes 4 servings.

PER SERVING: 206 CAL.; 4G PROT.; 4G FAT; 41G CARB.; 0 CHOL.; 16MG SOD.; 4G FIBER.
VEGAN

Ratatouille and Bean Stew

Salads & Sandwiches

Summer Veggie Melt, see page 33; Fruited Couscous Salad, see page 28

Fruited Couscous Salad

$^3/_4$ cup hot water
$^1/_8$ tsp. salt
$^1/_2$ cup uncooked couscous
$^1/_4$ cup frozen orange juice
    concentrate, thawed
1 Tbs. white wine vinegar
$1^1/_2$ tsp. sugar
$1^1/_2$ tsp. vegetable oil
$^1/_2$ tsp. grated orange peel

$^1/_2$ cup blueberries
$^1/_2$ cup red raspberries
$^1/_2$ cup hulled and halved
    strawberries
$^1/_2$ cup peach chunks ($^1/_2$-inch
    chunks)
$^1/_2$ cup plum chunks ($^1/_2$-inch
    chunks)
2 Tbs. fresh mint leaves

In a 1-quart saucepan, combine water and salt; bring to a boil over medium-high heat. Stir in couscous and cover. Remove from heat and let stand 5 minutes. Fluff couscous lightly with fork. Place in medium mixing bowl; set aside.

    In a 1-cup measure, combine juice concentrate, vinegar, sugar, oil and peel. Blend well with whisk. Add half of juice mixture to couscous; mix well. Cover and chill at least 1 hour.

    Add remaining juice mixture and remaining ingredients to couscous mixture. Toss gently to combine. Line serving bowl with lettuce, if desired. Makes 6 servings.

PER SERVING: 106 CAL.; 2G PROT.; 1G FAT; 22G CARB.; 0 CHOL.; 48MG SOD.; 2G FIBER.
VEGAN

Rio Verde Salad

$^2/_3$ cup uncooked wild rice
$^1/_2$ tsp. salt (optional)
1 Tbs. vegetable oil
1 medium green bell pepper,
    julienned
1 medium onion, sliced
8-oz. jar salsa

15-oz. can pinto or kidney beans,
    rinsed and drained
11-oz. can Mexican-style corn,
    drained
4 large lettuce leaves
$^1/_4$ cup cilantro leaves

Add wild rice to $2^2/_3$ cups boiling water. Add $^1/_2$ teaspoon salt per cup of rice, if desired; cover and simmer until grains are swollen and cracked down the sides, about 45 minutes to 1 hour.

    Heat oil in a large skillet. Add bell pepper and onion; sauté at medium-high heat until crisp-tender. Add salsa, beans, corn and wild rice; cook until heated through.

    Place $^1/_4$ of the mixture into each lettuce leaf. Sprinkle with cilantro. Makes 4 servings.

PER SERVING: 271 CAL.; 9G PROT.; 4G FAT; 49G CARB.; 0 CHOL.; 1,536MG SOD.; 8G FIBER.
VEGAN

Belgian Endive, Japanese Pear, Assorted Greens, Hazelnuts and Chèvre Salad

Chèvre Cream:
6 oz. chèvre (about $3/4$ cup), divided
2 Tbs. half-and-half
2 Tbs. water
Salt and pepper to taste

Endive:
4 heads Belgian endive
4 chives

Vinaigrette:
4 Tbs. olive oil
$1^1/3$ Tbs. balsamic vinegar
2 tsp. finely minced shallots
Salt and pepper to taste

Greens:
$1^1/2$ oz. frisé (about 1 cup lightly packed)
$1^1/2$ oz. watercress (about 1 cup lightly packed)
$1^1/2$ oz. red oakleaf lettuce, (about 1 cup lightly packed)

Garnishes:
32 roasted hazelnuts (optional)
4 dried apricots, julienned
1 Japanese pear, cut into about 30 small pieces

Combine 2 ounces chèvre, half-and-half and water in a food processor or blender; process until smooth. Season with salt and pepper. Pour mixture onto 4 plates; crumble remaining chèvre in center of each plate.

Finely julienne one head of endive; tie into a bundle with a chive. Repeat with remaining heads. Stand a bundle of endive upright in center of each plate. (If you can't get frisé or red oakleaf lettuce, substitute chicory, curly endive or romaine lettuce).

Whisk together vinaigrette ingredients; toss with remaining greens. Arrange around endive. Place 8 hazelnuts, if desired, and $1/4$ of the julienned apricots and pear pieces around edge of each plate. Makes 4 servings.

PER SERVING: 351CAL.; 6G PROT.; 28G FAT; 17G CARB.; 51MG CHOL.; 561MG SOD.; 4G FIBER. LACTO

Mandarin Salad with Tempeh

Marinade:
2 Tbs. low-sugar orange
    marmalade
1 tsp. minced ginger root
1 tsp. minced garlic
$^1/_4$ cup fresh lemon juice
$^1/_4$ cup rice vinegar
$^1/_4$ cup low-sodium soy sauce
$^1/_3$ cup fresh orange juice
$^1/_4$ tsp. cayenne pepper, or to taste

Salad:
1 lb. tempeh (any variety)
4 cups mixed fresh greens (such as
    curly endive, radicchio and
    leaf lettuce)
1 medium carrot, coarsely grated
1 cup thinly sliced fresh
    mushrooms
1 cup drained canned mandarin
    orange slices
$^1/_3$ to $^1/_2$ cup nonfat plain yogurt

Combine marinade ingredients in a shallow pan; set aside.

Cut tempeh into strips about 2 inches long and $^1/_2$ inch wide. Steam 20 minutes. Drain well; add to marinade. Cover and refrigerate; marinate at least 2 hours or overnight, occasionally basting tempeh with marinade.

In a large salad bowl, toss together greens, carrot, mushrooms and orange slices. Strain marinade from tempeh into a separate bowl. Toss tempeh with salad. Stir yogurt into marinade, adding more for a creamier texture; taste for seasoning, then toss with salad. Makes 6 servings.

Variation: For a lovely presentation, garnish perimeter of serving dish with slices of cooked beets.

PER SERVING: 235 CAL.; 15G PROT.; 5G FAT; 31G CARB.; <1MG CHOL.; 428MG SOD.; 6G FIBER.
LACTO

Falafel

Yogurt Sauce:
1 cup nonfat plain yogurt
$^1/_4$ tsp. salt
Pinch sugar
Black pepper to taste
1 Tbs. chopped fresh mint
      (1 tsp. dried)
2 cloves garlic

Hot Sauce:
1 cup vegetable broth
6 Tbs. tomato paste
2 tsp. red chili paste
1 Tbs. fresh lemon juice
$^1/_2$ tsp. ground cumin
1 Tbs. minced fresh parsley
      (1$^1/_2$ tsp. dried)
1 Tbs. minced cilantro (1$^1/_2$ tsp.
      dried coriander)

Falafel:
3 cloves garlic
$^1/_2$ medium onion, chopped
$^1/_2$ cup minced fresh parsley
1$^1/_2$ cups cooked garbanzo beans
1 Tbs. lemon juice
1 tsp. ground cumin
$^1/_2$ tsp. dried basil
$^1/_2$ tsp. ground coriander
$^1/_2$ tsp. dried thyme
$^1/_2$ tsp. salt
$^1/_2$ tsp. hot pepper sauce
Black pepper to taste
2 slices French bread, torn into
      large pieces and soaked in
      cold water to cover
$^1/_2$ cup whole wheat flour
1 Tbs. olive oil
4 whole wheat pita bread rounds

Yogurt Sauce: Combine all ingredients in a food processor or blender. Process until smooth; set aside.

Hot Sauce: Combine all ingredients in a small saucepan. Place over medium heat and simmer until thickened slightly, about 5 minutes.

Falafel: Preheat oven to 375 degrees. Blend garlic, onion and parsley in a food processor or blender until finely minced. Add garbanzos; blend until finely chopped and somewhat pasty. Add lemon juice, cumin, basil, coriander, thyme, salt, hot pepper sauce and black pepper. Squeeze water out of bread; add bread. Process until well mixed.

Form mixture into 16 balls. Flatten each ball to form $^1/_2$-inch thick patties; dredge in flour. Place patties on a lightly greased baking sheet. Bake 10 minutes. Turn and bake another 10 minutes.

In a large, heavy skillet, heat half the olive oil over medium-high heat. Add patties; fry until golden brown and crispy on bottom. Turn patties over and add remainder of oil, swirling it so that it comes into contact with all patties. Fry until golden brown and crispy; drain on paper towels.

To Serve: Cut off about $^1/_3$ of each pita round and open to form a pocket. Fill each pocket with 4 hot falafel patties. Serve with Yogurt Sauce and Hot Sauce. Makes 4 servings.

Variation: For a vegan sauce, omit yogurt from Yogurt Sauce and substitute half a 10$^1/_2$-oz. package of firm silken tofu plus $^1/_4$ cup lemon juice.

PER SERVING WITH 1 TBS. YOGURT SAUCE AND 1 TBS. HOT SAUCE: 386 CAL.; 15G PROT.; 7G FAT;
68G CARB.; <1MG CHOL.; 774MG SOD.; 10G FIBER.
LACTO/VEGAN

Warm New Potato Salad

Warm New Potato Salad

1 lb. new potatoes, cut into
    quarters (3 cups)
$3/4$ cup water
2 cups frozen broccoli, green
    beans, pearl onions and red
    pepper vegetable mixture

$1/3$ cup plain nonfat or low-fat
    yogurt
1 Tbs. snipped fresh Italian parsley
    or cilantro leaves
1 Tbs. Dijon mustard
$1/8$ tsp. salt

Combine potatoes and water in a 2-quart saucepan. Bring to a boil over high heat. Cover; reduce heat to low and simmer 15 to 20 minutes, or until potatoes are crisp-tender.

Stir in vegetable mixture. Cover and increase heat to medium-high. Cook 4 to 5 minutes, or until potatoes are tender and vegetables are hot, stirring occasionally. Drain; set aside.

Combine remaining ingredients in serving bowl. Add potato mixture and toss gently to coat. Serve warm. Makes 6 servings.

PER SERVING: 120 CAL.; 5G PROT.; <1G FAT; 25G CARB.; <1MG CHOL.; 352MG SOD.; 3G FIBER.
LACTO

Summer Veggie Melt

2 Tbs. lemon juice
1 Tbs. plus 1 tsp. Dijon mustard
2 tsp. canola oil
1 tsp. dried marjoram leaves
2 cups small fresh broccoli florets
16 small fresh asparagus spears,
    trimmed and cut in half
$3/4$ cup water
4 kaiser rolls, split

1 cup torn fresh spinach leaves
1 cup thinly sliced fresh mushrooms
$2/3$ cup thinly sliced zucchini or
    summer squash
$2/3$ cup alfalfa sprouts
4 thin red or green bell pepper
    rings
4 slices (1 oz. each) Provolone
    cheese

In a 1-cup measure, combine lemon juice, mustard, oil and marjoram; set aside. In a 3-quart saucepan, combine broccoli, asparagus and water. Cover and cook over high heat 5 to 7 minutes, or until vegetables are very hot and color brightens. Drain.

In a medium mixing bowl, combine broccoli mixture and half of dressing. Toss to combine; set aside. Brush cut side of each roll with remaining dressing. Arrange bottom halves of rolls on baking sheets.

Layer vegetables and sprouts evenly on roll halves. Top each with slice of cheese. Place under broiler with surface of cheese 4 to 5 inches from heat. Broil 1 to 2 minutes, or just until cheese is melted. Top with remaining roll halves. Makes 4 servings.

PER SANDWICH: 338 CAL.; 176 PROT.; 14G FAT; 39G CARB.; 19MG CHOL.; 733MG SOD.; 5G FIBER.
LACTO

Tacos

1 tsp. vegetable oil
1 small onion, finely chopped
³/4 tsp. curry powder
1 clove garlic, minced
2 tsp. dry mustard
28-oz. can tomatoes, chopped
    (include tomato liquid)
6 Tbs. salsa
3 Tbs. prepared horseradish
1 Tbs. apple cider vinegar

12 oz. firm tofu, frozen and
    thawed
¹/8 tsp. salt, or to taste
12 soft corn or wheat tortillas or
    commercial taco shells
Garnishes (optional): plain
    yogurt, shredded lettuce
    or other greens, grated
    cheddar or Monterey Jack
    cheese, chopped fresh
    tomatoes, sliced avocado

Heat oil in a large saucepan or skillet. Add onion; sauté 3 to 4 minutes. (For an oil-free version, sauté onion in some juice from tomatoes, or in vegetable stock or water.) Stir in curry powder, garlic and mustard; sauté briefly. Add tomatoes, salsa, horseradish and vinegar. Bring to a simmer, partially cover and cook about 1 hour, until sauce has thickened.

    Thoroughly squeeze moisture out of tofu; crumble into sauce. Continue to simmer sauce 30 minutes more, until tofu has absorbed the flavor of the sauce and sauce is desired consistency. Season with salt and additional vinegar, if desired.

    Heat tortillas or taco shells and fill with sauce and desired garnishes. Serve immediately. Makes 6 servings.

PER SERVING: 253 CAL.; 13G PROT.; 7G FAT; 33G CARB.; 0 CHOL.; 321MG SOD.; 4G FIBER.
VEGAN/LACTO

Tempeh Reuben Sandwiches

Sauce:
1 tsp. kudzu or arrowroot powder
1 tsp. cold water
1 Tbs. prepared mustard (preferably natural, stone-ground)
$3/4$ tsp. lemon juice
$1^1/2$ tsp. mellow barley miso
1 Tbs. sauerkraut liquid
6 Tbs. vegetable stock or water

Sandwich:
1 to 2 Tbs. vegetable oil
8 oz. tempeh
$1/2$ cup vegetable stock or water
8 slices rye or pumpernickel bread
16 lettuce leaves or other tender greens
4 green onions or shallots, finely chopped
1 tsp. minced fresh dill weed
2 cups well-drained sauerkraut

Sauce: Combine kudzu or arrowroot and cold water. Stir until dissolved. Add mustard, lemon juice, miso, sauerkraut liquid, and stock or water. Whisk until thoroughly combined; set aside.

Sandwich: Heat 1 tablespoon oil in a medium-sized skillet over moderate heat. Brown tempeh on one side. Turn and brown second side, adding more oil if necessary. Pour in stock or water and cover pan tightly. Cook until liquid is absorbed, turning tempeh once or twice. Remove skillet from heat and cut tempeh crosswise into strips about $1/4$-inch thick. Pour sauce over tempeh strips in skillet. Heat gently, stirring often, until sauce thickens and coats tempeh.

Lightly toast bread if desired. Place 2 lettuce leaves on each of 4 slices. Arrange $1/4$ of sauced tempeh strips on top of lettuce. Sprinkle $1/4$ of green onion and dill over tempeh. Top each with $1/2$ cup sauerkraut, 2 more lettuce leaves and a slice of bread. Serve immediately. Makes 4 sandwiches.

PER SANDWICH: 484 CAL.; 25G PROT.; 13G FAT; 54G CARB.; 0 CHOL.; 1,773MG SOD.; 10G FIBER.
VEGAN

Potato-Mushroom Burgers

Potato-Mushroom Burgers

$^3/_4$ cup finely chopped
   mushrooms
4 green onions, thinly sliced
3 cloves garlic, minced
1 to 2 Tbs. canola oil
$^1/_2$ cup unsalted raw cashews
$2^1/_2$ cups mashed potatoes

$^3/_4$ cup grated carrots
2 tsp. grated ginger root
Salt and pepper to taste
1 egg white (or $^1/_4$ cup dry bread
   crumbs)
$^1/_2$ cup sesame seeds, or to taste

In a 10-inch nonstick skillet, combine mushrooms, green onions, garlic
and oil. Cook over medium heat 5 minutes or until vegetables are tender,
stirring occasionally.

    Meanwhile, place cashews in a blender or food processor; grind to a
coarse meal. In a large bowl, combine mushroom mixture, ground cashews,
potatoes, carrots, ginger, and salt and pepper. Add egg white; mix well.
(The mixture will be soft and moist.)

    Place sesame seeds in a shallow dish. Shape $^1/_2$ cup potato mixture into
$3^1/_2$-inch patty. Carefully press both sides of patty into sesame seeds, coat-
ing generously. Repeat with remaining potato mixture and sesame seeds.

    Spray a 12-inch nonstick skillet with vegetable cooking spray. Heat
skillet over medium heat. Cook patties until golden brown on both sides,
about 5 minutes per side. Makes 6 patties.

    Variation: Sauté burgers in olive oil until golden brown.

PER BURGER: 246 CAL.; 6G PROT.; 15G FAT; 23G CARB.; 0 CHOL.; 23MG SOD.; 4G FIBER.
OVO-LACTO/VEGAN

Legumes

Black Bean Quesadillas, see page 40

Black Bean Quesadillas

15-oz. can black beans, rinsed and
drained
1/4 cup chopped green or
red tomato
3 Tbs. chopped cilantro
12 black olives, pitted and
thinly sliced

8 6-inch sprouted wheat or whole
wheat tortillas
4 oz. shredded jalapeño-jack cheese
or soy cheese
32 spinach leaves, stemmed and
finely shredded
4 Tbs. hot salsa

Mash beans in a large bowl. Stir in tomato, cilantro and olives. Spread bean mixture evenly onto 4 tortillas. Sprinkle with cheese, spinach and salsa. Top with remaining tortillas to make sandwiches.

Preheat oven to 350 degrees. Place tortillas on an ungreased baking sheet and bake 12 minutes, or until cheese melts. Or, cook on a cast-iron griddle over medium heat, turning once, until cheese melts. Cut into wedges and serve hot. Makes 4 servings.

PER SERVING: 443 CAL.; 21G PROT.; 14G FAT; 56G CARB.; 25MG CHOL.; 646MG SOD.; 8G FIBER.
LACTO/VEGAN

TIP: Depending on your cheese and bean choices, you can really get creative with this Tex-Mex inspired sandwich: sharp cheddar with scarlet runner beans, and mozzarella with anasazi beans are great variations. Sprouted wheat and whole wheat tortillas are available at natural food stores.

Pink Beans with Marinated Seitan

1 lb. seitan, julienned
$1/4$ cup tamari or soy sauce
$1/4$ cup olive oil
$1/3$ cup fresh lime juice
1 large clove garlic, minced
1 tsp. salt, or to taste
$1/2$ tsp. pepper, or to taste
$1/2$ tsp. ground cumin
12 cups finely shredded lettuce

2 16-oz. cans pinto or light red
   kidney beans, drained and
   rinsed
1 large red bell pepper, julienned
$1/4$ cup cilantro or parsley and
   seeds from red bell pepper
   for garnish (optional)

In a heavy skillet, combine seitan, and tamari or soy sauce. Bring to a simmer and cook, stirring frequently, until liquid is absorbed. Remove from heat. Set aside to cool.

In a large bowl, combine olive oil, lime juice, garlic, salt, pepper and cumin; mix well. Stir in cooked seitan. Marinate at least 15 minutes, or cover and refrigerate overnight. Remove from refrigerator at least 1 hour before assembling rest of salad.

To assemble, place lettuce in large serving bowl, spread seitan mixture on top, add beans and red bell pepper strips. Toss lightly. Garnish with parsley and red bell pepper seeds, if desired. Makes 6 servings.

PER SERVING: 393 CAL.; 25G PROT.; 11G FAT; 67G CARB.; 0 CHOL.; 1,404MG SOD.; 9G FIBER.
VEGAN

No-Guilt Refried Beans

No-Guilt Refried Beans

16-oz. can pinto beans, rinsed and drained
1/4 cup thick and chunky salsa
2 Tbs. finely chopped onion
1/8 tsp. garlic powder
1 Tbs. margarine

Combine beans, salsa, onion and garlic powder in a 2-quart saucepan. Bring mixture to a boil over medium-high heat, stirring occasionally. Reduce heat to medium-low. Simmer 7 to 10 minutes, or until onion is translucent, stirring occasionally. Add margarine; stir until melted.

In a food processor or blender, process mixture until smooth. Serve as a taco ingredient or chip and vegetable dip. Makes 4 servings.

PER SERVING: 123 CAL.; 5G PROT.; 3G FAT; 18G CARB.; 3MG CHOL.; 675MG SOD.; 6G FIBER.
LACTO/VEGAN

Tri-Bean Bake

1 small onion, thinly sliced
1/4 cup thinly sliced celery
1 tsp. vegetable oil
1 cup cooked pinto beans
1 cup cooked butter (lima) beans
1 cup cooked garbanzo beans
2/3 cup tomato sauce
1/4 cup frozen apple juice concentrate, defrosted
1 Tbs. light molasses (optional)
1/2 tsp. dry mustard

Preheat oven to 375 degrees. In a 10-inch nonstick skillet, combine onion, celery and oil. Cook over medium heat 5 to 8 minutes, or until vegetables are tender, stirring occasionally. Remove from heat. Stir in remaining ingredients.

Spoon mixture into 1-quart casserole. Cover and bake 25 to 30 minutes, or until hot and bubbly. Makes 6 servings.

PER SERVING: 169 CAL.; 8G PROT.; 2G FAT; 32G CARB.; 0 CHOL.; 176MG SOD.; 7G FIBER.
VEGAN

Mediterranean Pot Stickers

2 cups cooked lentils
$^1/_3$ cup crumbled feta cheese
$^1/_4$ cup finely chopped onion
1 Tbs. snipped fresh dill weed
1 clove garlic, minced
$^1/_2$ tsp. grated lemon peel

$^1/_4$ tsp. pepper
12 7-inch square egg roll wrappers
2 Tbs. water
2 tsp. olive oil
$^1/_2$ cup hot water
Dollop plain yogurt (optional)

Combine lentils, feta, onion, dill, garlic, lemon peel and pepper in a medium mixing bowl; set aside.

Cut a 6-inch circle from each egg roll skin. (Use inverted 1$^1/_2$-pint mixing bowl as template.) Cover egg roll skins with plastic wrap to prevent drying. Place 2 tablespoons lentil mixture on bottom half of 1 circle, $^1/_4$ inch from edge.

Brush edges lightly with water. Fold top half over, pressing with fingers to seal. Bring the corners of half-circle together, overlapping slightly. Brush lightly with water to seal. (Keep pot stickers covered.) Repeat with remaining filling and egg roll skins.

Spray a 12-inch nonstick skillet with vegetable cooking spray. Heat oil over medium heat; add pot stickers. Cook 2 to 3 minutes, or until bottoms of pot stickers are light golden brown. Add hot water. Cover and reduce heat to medium-low. Simmer 8 to 10 minutes, or until water boils off and bottoms of pot stickers are golden brown. Serve warm with a dollop of plain yogurt, if desired. Makes 6 servings.

PER SERVING: 173 CAL.; 9G PROT.; 5G FAT; 24G CARB.; 13MG CHOL.; 234MG SOD.; 5G FIBER.
OVO-LACTO

Lima Bean Succotash

2 tsp. olive oil, divided
2 green bell peppers, chopped
2 medium red or white potatoes,
    cut into $1/2$-inch cubes
3 stalks celery, sliced
2 tsp. fresh thyme leaves
    (1 tsp. dried)
2 tsp. fresh marjoram leaves
    (1 tsp. dried)
$1/2$ tsp. asafetida or 1 clove garlic,
    minced

3 cups cooked lima (butter)
    beans, drained (reserve
    liquid)
2 cups fresh or frozen corn kernels
Salt and pepper to taste
$1/4$ cup nonfat sour cream or
    soymilk
3 Tbs. snipped fresh parsley

In a 4-quart heavy saucepan, heat 1 teaspoon oil over medium heat. Add bell peppers, potatoes, celery, thyme, marjoram and asafetida or garlic; stir-fry 3 minutes.

    Add enough water to reserved bean liquid to make 3 cups and add to pepper mixture. Bring to a boil over high heat. Reduce heat to low and simmer 15 minutes. Stir in beans and corn; simmer 5 minutes, or until hot. Add salt and pepper to taste. Remove from heat.

    Stir in sour cream or soymilk, and parsley. To serve, garnish with additional chopped parsley and remaining olive oil. Makes 6 servings.

PER SERVING: 283 CAL.; 10G PROT.; 5G FAT; 53G CARB.; 0 CHOL.; 55MG SOD.; 8G FIBER.
LACTO/VEGAN

Garbanzo Bean and Vegetable Pie

Garbanzo Bean and Vegetable Pie

2 cups seeded chopped tomatoes
1 1/2 cups thinly sliced yellow
    summer squash
1 1/2 cups thinly sliced zucchini
    squash
1 cup sliced fresh mushrooms
1/2 cup chopped onion
1 tsp. dried basil leaves
1/2 tsp. salt, divided

15-oz. can garbanzo beans, rinsed
    and drained
1/2 cup shredded hard farmer
    cheese (2 oz.), divided
1 cup vegetable broth
1 cup uncooked couscous
2 egg whites
1/4 cup snipped fresh parsley

Preheat oven to 350 degrees. Spray a 10-inch deep-dish pie plate with vegetable cooking spray; set aside.

In a 3-quart saucepan, combine tomatoes, squashes, mushrooms, onion, basil and 1/4 teaspoon salt. Cook over medium heat 8 to 10 minutes, or until vegetables are tender, stirring occasionally. Remove from heat. Add beans and 1/4 cup cheese. Mix well; set aside.

In a 1-quart saucepan, combine broth and remaining 1/4 teaspoon salt. Bring to a boil over medium-high heat. Stir in couscous, cover and remove from heat. Let stand 5 minutes. Fluff couscous lightly with fork. Add egg whites and parsley to couscous; mix well.

Using the back of a spoon, press couscous mixture into bottom and up sides of prepared pie plate. Spoon vegetable mixture into couscous crust. Bake 25 to 30 minutes, or until crust is firm and filling is hot. Sprinkle top of pie with remaining 1/4 cup cheese. Let stand until cheese is melted. Serve hot in wedges. Makes 6 to 8 servings.

PER SERVING: 255 CAL.; 14G PROT.; 3G FAT; 44G CARB.; 5MG CHOL.; 561MG SOD.; 7G FIBER.
OVO-LACTO

Pasta, Rice & Grains

Garlic and Tomato Risotto, see page 50

Garlic and Tomato Risotto

1 medium onion, finely chopped
1 medium red bell pepper,
    finely chopped
3 Tbs. minced garlic
1 Tbs. chopped sun-dried tomatoes
    (without oil)
1 cup chopped and drained fresh
    or canned tomatoes
1 to 2 tsp. dried basil leaves

$^1/_2$ tsp. dried oregano leaves
2 cups uncooked arborio rice
5 to 7 cups hot vegetable broth
2 cups chopped fresh spinach
    leaves
1 Tbs. Parmesan cheese (optional)
Salt and pepper to taste

Spray a 3-quart saucepan or 12-inch nonstick skillet with vegetable cooking spray. Heat over medium-high heat. Add onion; sauté until soft but not browned. (Add $^1/_4$ cup vegetable broth if needed to prevent onion from browning.) Add bell pepper, garlic, dried and fresh tomatoes, basil and oregano. Sauté, stirring about 5 minutes.

Add rice; sauté 1 minute. Pour in $^1/_2$ cup broth. Bring to a boil; reduce heat to medium. Cook, stirring constantly, until liquid is almost completely absorbed. Add another $^1/_2$ cup broth. Continue stirring and adding broth $^1/_2$ cup at a time as it is absorbed.

Stop adding broth when rice is creamy and just tender, about 30 to 35 minutes. Remove risotto from heat and stir in spinach. Add Parmesan cheese, if desired, and salt and pepper to taste. Serve immediately. Makes 6 servings.

PER SERVING: 279 CAL.; 6G PROT.; 1G FAT; 60G CARB.; 0 CHOL.; 33MG SOD.; 5G FIBER.
VEGAN/LACTO

Tabbouleh-Stuffed Avocados

$^1/_2$ cup boiling water
$^1/_4$ cup uncooked bulgur (cracked
    wheat)
1 small tomato, seeded and finely
    chopped ($^1/_2$ cup)
$^1/_2$ cup snipped fresh parsley
$^1/_4$ cup thinly sliced green onions

Dressing:
1 to 2 Tbs. lemon juice
1 Tbs. olive oil
$^1/_4$ tsp. salt

2 ripe avocados, cut in half
    lengthwise

Place water in a 2-cup measure; stir in bulgur. Let stand 30 minutes. Drain, pressing with back of spoon to remove excess moisture.

In a medium mixing bowl, combine bulgur, tomato, parsley and onions. In a separate bowl, combine dressing ingredients. Add dressing to bulgur mixture; toss to coat. Spoon salad evenly into avocado halves and serve immediately. Makes 4 servings.

PER SERVING: 222 CAL.; 3G PROT.; 19G FAT; 15G CARB.; 0 CHOL.; 152MG SOD.; 4G FIBER.
VEGAN

Mushroom Stroganoff

1 oz. dried shiitake mushrooms
1 1/2 cups boiling water
8 oz. medium or firm tofu
1/2 tsp. salt
2 Tbs. lemon juice
2 Tbs. canola oil or safflower oil
1 Tbs. plus 1 tsp. tahini
2 Tbs. water or sesame oil
2 medium onions, finely chopped
1 lb. domestic white mushrooms,
    thickly sliced (about 3 cups)

Freshly ground black pepper to taste
1/2 tsp. paprika, plus more if desired
1/4 cup plus 2 Tbs. dry red wine
2 Tbs. soy sauce
1 tsp. fresh thyme leaves
2 Tbs. minced fresh dill weed,
    or to taste
3 cups cooked buckwheat groats,
    brown rice or wide noodles
2 Tbs. minced fresh parsley

In a small bowl, combine shiitake mushrooms and boiling water. Cover; set aside to soak 1 to 2 hours. Squeeze liquid out of mushrooms; cut off and discard tough stems. Slice caps as thinly as possible. Reserve mushroom-soaking liquid.

Combine tofu, salt, lemon juice, oil and tahini in a food processor or blender. Process until smooth; set aside. Heat water or sesame oil in a large nonstick skillet. Add onion; sauté until almost tender, about 3 minutes. Add sliced shiitakes and white mushrooms, pepper and paprika; continue to sauté about 5 minutes, or until fresh mushrooms no longer appear dry. Add 1/2 cup reserved mushroom-soaking liquid, wine and soy sauce. Cover and cook over low heat 5 minutes, until mushrooms are tender and flavors are blended.

Stir in tofu mixture, thyme and dill weed. Cook briefly until slightly thickened. Serve over hot groats, rice or noodles. Garnish with parsley and additional paprika, if desired. Makes 4 servings.

Variation: Substitute 1/4 teaspoon dried thyme leaves and 1 teaspoon dried dill weed for fresh. Add thyme to sauté along with pepper and paprika; add dill weed near end of cooking.

PER SERVING: 413 CAL.; 20G PROT.; 16G FAT; 52G CARB.; 0 CHOL.; 767MG SOD.; 8G FIBER.
VEGAN

TIP: Dried herbs and spices lose their flavor and potency after about a year. It is best to buy them in the smallest possible amounts and store in tightly closed bottles in a cool, dry spot out of direct light.

Fresh Noodles Lo Mein

Fresh Noodles Lo Mein

1 Tbs. dark sesame oil
$^1/_2$ lb. firm tofu, cut into 1-inch
    cubes
4 vegetable bouillon cubes (or
    equivalent in instant broth
    powder; see note)
4 cups cold water
1 Tbs. grated ginger root
$^1/_8$ tsp. crushed red pepper
    (optional)

3 Tbs. bottled teriyaki sauce
1 large clove garlic, minced
8-oz. package fresh linguine
16-oz. bag frozen Oriental-style
    vegetables
1 small onion, sliced lengthwise
    into petals
2 scallions, finely sliced

Heat sesame oil in a skillet over medium-high heat. Sauté tofu until golden on all sides, about 2 to 3 minutes. In a large stockpot, bring bouillon or broth powder and water to a boil. Add ginger, pepper if desired, teriyaki sauce, garlic and linguine. Simmer 2 minutes. Stir in browned tofu, vegetables and onion; return to a boil and simmer 2 more minutes. Stir in sliced scallions. Makes 6 servings.

Note: Use a quantity of instant broth powder indicated on the package to make 4 cups of liquid broth.

Variation: Used dried linguine or other pasta instead of fresh, and increase the boiling time to cook pasta until al dente (firm).

PER SERVING: 230 CAL.; 12G PROT.; 6G FAT; 30G CARB.; 62MG CHOL.; 432MG SOD.; 4G FIBER.
VEGAN

TIP: Rice, pasta and beans can be cooked in quantity ahead of time. Package them in meal-size portions and freeze. Thaw a container in the refrigerator during the day so it is ready to reheat at mealtime. Pasta needs only a brief dip in boiling water.

Swedish Wheat Balls

1 cup bulgur
3 cups cold water
2 Tbs. water
1 small onion, finely chopped
2 tsp. red miso or salt to taste
$^1/_4$ cup evaporated skim milk or
      soymilk
1 tsp. vegetable seasoning, such as
      Spike or Vegesal
1 medium boiled potato, mashed

3 Tbs. fine bread crumbs,
      preferably whole grain
$^1/_4$ cup egg substitute, 1 egg or
      equivalent Egg Replacer
$^1/_4$ tsp. pepper
Pinch nutmeg
1 Tbs. finely minced parsley leaves
1 Tbs. butter or margarine
1 Tbs. canola oil

Combine bulgur and water; set aside 30 minutes to allow bulgur to expand. Drain; with hands, press out as much water as possible. Transfer bulgur to a large mixing bowl.

While bulgur soaks, spray a small skillet with vegetable cooking spray. Add 2 tablespoons water and onion; sauté until water evaporates and onion becomes translucent, about 3 minutes. Remove from heat. Add miso or salt, and milk to onion mixture; blend well. Blend in vegetable seasoning.

Add onion mixture, potato, bread crumbs, egg substitute, pepper, nutmeg and parsley to bulgur. Blend thoroughly. Shape into small balls about 2 inches in diameter; arrange in a single layer on a tray. Cover with plastic wrap and chill at least 1 hour before continuing.

Preheat oven to 300 degrees. In a large skillet over high heat, heat butter and oil together. Add 8 to 10 wheat balls; sauté over moderate heat on all sides until lightly browned, about 5 minutes. Continue sautéing until all wheat balls are browned. Transfer to a baking dish. Bake 15 minutes. Makes about 30 wheat balls, about 6 servings.

Variation: If serving as a main course, make a sauce to serve over wide noodles: In hot drippings left in sauté pan, combine $^3/_4$ cup evaporated milk, $^1/_4$ cup cold water, 2 tablespoons potato starch, 1 teaspoon salt, $^1/_4$ teaspoon white pepper and a pinch nutmeg. Bring to a simmer, whisking until sauce comes to a boil and thickens. Serve over wheat balls and noodles.

PER SERVING: 109 CAL.; 4G PROT.; 2G FAT; 18G CARB.; 3MG CHOL.; 55MG SOD.; 2G FIBER.
OVO-LACTO/VEGAN

Swedish Wheat Balls

Pasta Pizza

8 oz. uncooked capellini (angel
    hair pasta)
1 Tbs. plus 1 tsp. olive oil, divided
$^1/_3$ cup chopped green bell pepper
$^1/_4$ cup chopped onion

$1^1/_4$ cups low-fat pasta sauce
$^1/_4$ cup sliced black olives (optional)
$^1/_2$ cup shredded part-skim or
    nonfat mozzarella cheese
$^1/_4$ tsp. Italian seasoning

Prepare capellini as directed on package. Rinse and drain; set aside.

In a 6-inch nonstick skillet, combine 1 teaspoon oil, bell pepper and onion. Cook over medium-high heat 3 to 5 minutes, or until vegetables are tender, stirring frequently; set aside.

Heat remaining oil over medium-high heat in a 10-inch nonstick skillet. Spread capellini in skillet and cook until lightly browned on underside, about 4 to 6 minutes. Turn pasta crust onto plate. Slip crust back into skillet browned side up and reduce heat to medium.

Spoon sauce evenly over crust. Top evenly with prepared vegetables and olives, if desired, and sprinkle with cheese and Italian seasoning. Cover and cook until cheese is melted, about 4 to 5 minutes. Cut pizza into wedges. Makes 6 servings.

PER SLICE: 219 CAL.; 8G PROT.; 5G FAT; 34G CARB.; 3MG CHOL.; 236MG SOD.; 3G FIBER.
LACTO

Pasta Pizza

Vegetable Lasagna

(pictured on cover)

6 uncooked lasagna noodles
1 cup shredded carrots
1 cup green and red bell pepper
    strips (2- by $^1/_4$-inch strips)
$^1/_2$ cup chopped onion
$^1/_4$ cup dry red wine
1 clove garlic, minced
$1^1/_2$ cups frozen broccoli cuts,
    thawed and drained
$14^1/_2$-oz. can diced tomatoes,
    drained

$^1/_4$ cup snipped fresh basil leaves
15-oz. carton light ricotta cheese
$^1/_3$ cup snipped fresh parsley
1 egg white
$2^3/_4$ cups prepared marinara sauce
    or seasoned tomato sauce
1 cup shredded reduced-fat
    mozzarella cheese

Heat oven to 350 degrees. Spray 8- by 8-inch baking dish with vegetable cooking spray; set aside. Prepare lasagna noodles as directed on package. Rinse and let stand in warm water.

In a 10-inch nonstick skillet, combine carrots, bell pepper strips, onion, wine and garlic. Cook over medium heat 7 to 9 minutes, or until vegetables are tender, stirring occasionally. Add broccoli, tomatoes and basil. Mix well and set aside. In a small mixing bowl, combine ricotta, parsley and egg white.

Drain noodles and cut as necessary to fit dish. Spread $^1/_2$ cup marinara sauce in bottom of prepared dish. Cover with 2 noodles, then $^1/_2$ cup sauce, $^1/_3$ ricotta mixture, $^1/_3$ vegetable mixture and $^1/_4$ cup mozzarella cheese. Repeat layers with noodles, sauce, ricotta mixture, vegetable mixture and mozzarella. Top with remaining $^3/_4$ cup sauce.

Bake 45 to 50 minutes, or until hot and bubbly around edges. Sprinkle with remaining $^1/_4$ cup mozzarella cheese. Bake 5 to 10 minutes, or until cheese is melted. Let stand 10 minutes before serving. Makes 6 servings.

PER SERVING: 367 CAL.; 24G PROT.; 12G FAT; 46G CARB.; 19MG CHOL.; 1,109MG SOD.; 7G FIBER.
OVO-LACTO

Jolof Rice

1 cup dry black-eyed peas
2 medium eggplants
1 tsp. salt
1$^1/_2$ Tbs. canola oil
2 large onions, chopped
3 Tbs. chopped ginger root
2 jalapeño peppers, stems and
    seeds removed, roasted
    and chopped
1 whole clove garlic

1 green bell pepper, chopped
2 cloves garlic, minced
4 large tomatoes, chopped
1$^1/_2$ Tbs. tomato paste
2 tsp. cayenne
2 tsp. curry powder
Hot pepper sauce to taste (optional)
1 lb. carrots, chopped (about 3 cups)
1$^1/_2$ cups long-grain brown rice
$^1/_2$ lb. green beans, cut in thirds

Soak peas overnight; drain. Simmer in about 2 quarts fresh water 15 minutes. Drain and reserve cooking water. Slice eggplants in rounds about $^1/_2$ inch thick; place in a colander. Sprinkle with salt and let drain 5 minutes.

Heat oil in an ovenproof pan or casserole. Brown eggplant with 1 tablespoon chopped onion, 1 tablespoon chopped ginger, 1 chopped jalapeño, 1 whole clove garlic and bell pepper about 5 minutes. Remove eggplant from pan; set aside. Add remaining onion, ginger, jalapeño, garlic, bean liquid, tomatoes, tomato paste, cayenne, curry powder and hot pepper sauce, if desired; simmer 10 minutes. Add peas, carrots and rice; simmer 5 minutes more. Add green beans and browned eggplant. Simmer 15 minutes more.

Cover and bake in a 400-degree oven 25 to 30 minutes. Makes 6 servings.

PER SERVING: 411 CAL.; 11G PROT.; 4G FAT; 80G CARB.; 0 CHOL.; 415MG SOD.; 17G FIBER.
VEGAN

Green Rice with Spinach

$1^1/_2$ Tbs. canola oil
1 medium onion, diced
2 cloves garlic, minced
1 green bell pepper, seeded and
    diced
1 jalapeño pepper, seeded and
    minced
2 cups water

1 cup long-grain white or brown
    rice
1 Tbs. dried parsley
1 tsp. ground cumin
$^1/_2$ tsp. salt
$^1/_4$ tsp. black pepper
2 cups chopped fresh spinach
2 Tbs. minced fresh cilantro

In a large saucepan or Dutch oven, heat oil. Add onion, garlic, bell pepper and jalapeño; sauté 5 to 7 minutes, or until onions are tender. Add water, rice, parsley, cumin, salt and pepper; cover.

Simmer over medium heat about 15 minutes (40 minutes if using brown rice). Stir in spinach and cilantro; cook over low heat about 5 minutes more, until rice is tender. Makes 4 servings.

PER SERVING: 188 CAL.; 3G PROT.; 5G FAT; 31G CARB.; 0 CHOL.; 442MG SOD.; 3G FIBER.
VEGAN

TIP: Peppers aren't just fiery to the tongue; capsaicin (the flavorless, colorless chemical that makes peppers hot) can also burn your skin and eyes. When handling and preparing peppers, it is wise to wear plastic or rubber gloves, because the capsaicin can remain on your hands for hours, even after washing.

Rice and Vegetable Croquettes

$^1/_3$ cup diced red bell pepper
$^1/_4$ cup shredded carrot
$^1/_4$ cup sliced green onions
$1^1/_2$ cups cooked brown rice
2 egg whites

1 Tbs. all-purpose flour
$^1/_4$ tsp. dried thyme leaves
$^1/_4$ tsp. salt

Spray a 12-inch nonstick skillet with vegetable cooking spray. Add bell pepper, carrot and onions. Cook over medium heat 5 to 8 minutes, or until vegetables are crisp-tender, stirring frequently. (If vegetables begin to stick, move them to one side and spray skillet again.) Remove from heat. Cool slightly.

In a medium mixing bowl, combine vegetable mixture and remaining ingredients. Wipe skillet with paper towel, and spray with vegetable cooking spray. Heat skillet over medium heat.

Drop $^1/_3$ cup rice mixture into skillet, flattening with back of spatula to form $3^1/_2$-inch patty. Repeat with remaining rice mixture. Cook 4 to 7 minutes, or until light golden brown, turning patties over once. Makes 6 croquettes.

PER CROQUETTE: 70 CAL.; 3G PROT.; <1G FAT; 13G CARB.; 0 CHOL.; 112MG SOD.; 1G FIBER.
OVO-LACTO

Polenta Rounds with Sautéed Vegetables and Gremolada

Polenta Rounds with Sautéed Vegetables and Gremolada

Polenta:
3 cups water
1 Tbs. butter or soy margarine
$^3/_4$ tsp. salt
1 cup stone-ground yellow
    cornmeal
1 cup cold water
Melted butter or soy margarine

Gremolada:
2 tsp. minced lemon zest
1 tsp. minced garlic
2 Tbs. minced cilantro or parsley

Vegetables:
1 to 2 Tbs. olive oil
$^1/_4$ cup sliced onion
6 oz. thin asparagus spears, cut into
    2-inch lengths
2 medium carrots, pared and cut
    into thick matchsticks
2 small zucchini, cut into thick
    matchsticks
2 small yellow squash, cut into
    thick matchsticks
1 small red bell pepper, cored, halved
    and cut into thick strips
$^1/_2$ cup small sliced cremini or
    white button mushrooms
2 tsp. lemon juice

Polenta: In a heavy 2-quart saucepan over medium heat, bring 3 cups water to a boil with butter or margarine, and salt. In a small bowl, combine cornmeal with 1 cup cold water. Slowly pour cornmeal mixture into boiling water, stirring constantly. Return to boiling (mixture will begin to pop), then reduce heat. Cook, uncovered, stirring frequently, about 10 minutes or until mixture begins to mound onto itself when dropped from spoon. Spoon mixture into six 4- by $^1/_2$-inch tart pans with removable bottoms. Cover and chill until firm, preferably overnight.

When ready to serve, unmold polenta rounds from tart pans. Place on an unheated broiler pan. Brush tops and sides of polenta lightly with melted butter or margarine. Broil 4 inches from heat about 8 to 10 minutes on each side, or until browned and crisp, brushing again after turning.

Gremolada: Combine lemon zest, garlic, and cilantro or parsley in a small bowl; set aside.

Vegetables: Heat oil over medium-high heat in a large deep skillet. Add onion, asparagus and carrots. Cook, stirring frequently, 3 minutes. Add zucchini, yellow squash, bell pepper and mushrooms. Cook, stirring frequently, until vegetables are crisp-tender and mushrooms have softened, about 4 to 5 minutes. Sprinkle with lemon juice and gremolada; toss gently to combine. Spoon over polenta rounds. Makes 6 servings.

Variation: For a more decorative dish, steam whole asparagus spears and serve on the side.

PER SERVING: 153 CAL.; 3G PROT.; 4G FAT; 25G CARB.; 5MG CHOL.; 301MG SOD.; 4G FIBER.
LACTO/VEGAN

Vegetables

Potato Medley, see page 66

Potato Medley

5 russet potatoes (5 to 6 oz. each), peeled and cut into $^1/_2$-inch cubes
$1^1/_2$ cups water
1 Tbs. canola oil
2 cups chopped broccoli
1 red bell pepper, seeded and diced
1 green bell pepper, seeded and diced
1 cup frozen peas, defrosted
2 green onions, finely chopped
2 cloves garlic, minced
1 tsp. dried oregano or rosemary leaves
1 tsp. dried basil leaves
Salt, black pepper and crushed red pepper flakes to taste

In a 3-quart saucepan, combine potatoes and water. Cover and cook over medium-high heat 10 to 12 minutes, or just until potatoes are tender. Drain.

In a 12-inch nonstick skillet, heat oil over medium heat. Add potatoes and remaining ingredients. Sauté 6 to 8 minutes, until potatoes become slightly creamy and vegetables are crisp-tender. Makes 6 servings.

PER SERVING: 156 CAL.; 5G PROT.; 3G FAT; 30G CARB.; 0 CHOL.; 38MG SOD.; 5G FIBER.
VEGAN

Hasselback Potatoes

6 baking potatoes (5 to 6 oz. each), about 4 inches long and 2 inches wide
Butter-flavored vegetable spray
2 Tbs. melted margarine or butter
1 tsp. kosher or regular salt
2 Tbs. unseasoned dry bread crumbs
2 Tbs. grated hard cheese (any kind)
Vegetable seasoning, lemon pepper, seasoned salt, margarine or butter to taste (optional)

Preheat oven to 425 degrees. Place 1 potato at a time on a wooden spoon large enough to cradle it comfortably. Beginning about $^1/_2$ inch from one end, slice down crosswise at $^1/_8$-inch intervals without cutting through the potato. (Bowl of spoon should prevent knife from slicing completely through potato.) Place in a large bowl of cold water to prevent discoloring. Drain potatoes; pat dry.

Generously spray a 12- by 8-inch baking dish with vegetable spray. Arrange potatoes cut side up and drizzle with melted margarine or butter. Sprinkle with salt; set pan in middle of oven. Bake 30 minutes.

Sprinkle bread crumbs over potatoes and baste with melted margarine from bottom of pan, adding butter-flavored spray if needed. Bake another 20 minutes or until potatoes are fork-tender. Sprinkle potatoes with cheese and seasonings. Bake 3 to 5 minutes, or until cheese is melted. Makes 6 servings.

PER SERVING: 198 CAL.; 4G PROT.; 5G FAT; 35G CARB.; 6MG CHOL.; 457MG SOD.; 2G FIBER.
LACTO

Tamale Pie

Filling:
- 16-oz. can whole tomatoes, drained and cut up
- 2 cups frozen corn
- 15-oz. can pinto beans, rinsed and drained
- 4 oz. chopped green chilies
- 1/3 cup chopped green bell pepper
- 1/3 cup chopped onion
- 1/2 tsp. ground cumin
- 1/2 tsp. chili powder
- 1/4 tsp. dried cilantro leaves
- 1/4 tsp. dried oregano leaves
- 1/4 tsp. garlic powder

Crust:
- 1/4 cup yellow cornmeal
- 1/2 cup all-purpose flour
- 1 tsp. baking powder
- 1 Tbs. sugar
- 1/4 tsp. salt
- 1/2 cup skim milk
- 1/4 cup egg substitute, or 1 egg
- 1 Tbs. vegetable oil
- Dash paprika (optional)

- Fresh red or jalapeño pepper to garnish(optional)

Preheat oven to 350 degrees. In a 3-quart saucepan, combine filling ingredients. Cook over medium heat, stirring occasionally, 10 to 15 minutes, or until mixure is very hot and flavors are blended. Cover to keep warm; set aside.

Combine cornmeal, flour, baking powder, sugar and salt in small mixing bowl. Add remaining ingredients. Mix just until batter is blended.

Spoon filling into a 9-inch round cake dish. Spoon batter over filling. Sprinkle top with paprika, if desired. Bake 30 to 40 minutes, or until cornmeal crust is golden brown. Let stand 10 minutes. Garnish with fresh red pepper or jalapeño pepper, if desired. Makes 6 servings.

PER SERVING: 214 CAL.; 9G PROT.; 3G FAT; 41G CARB.; <1MG CHOL.; 758MG SOD.; 6G FIBER.
OVO-LACTO

Potato and Chive Turnovers with Sweet Carrot Salsa

Salsa:
1 cup diced carrots
$^1/_3$ cup diced green bell pepper
1 Tbs. olive oil
$^1/_3$ cup sliced green onions
2 Tbs. packed brown sugar
1 Tbs. white vinegar
1 Tbs. catsup
1 clove garlic, minced
$^1/_4$ tsp. cayenne pepper

Filling:
6 small red potatoes ($2^1/_2$ to 3 oz.
    each), peeled
4 cups water
$^1/_3$ cup Parmesan cheese
2 Tbs. shredded carrot
2 tsp. snipped fresh chives
$^1/_4$ tsp. salt
6 egg roll wrappers, trimmed into
    6-inch squares
$^1/_4$ cup vegetable oil

In a 1-quart saucepan, combine carrots, bell pepper and olive oil. Cook over medium heat 5 to 7 minutes, or until carrots are tender, stirring frequently. Remove from heat. Add remaining salsa ingredients. Mix well and cover. Chill at least 2 hours.

In a 2-quart saucepan, combine potatoes and water. Bring to a boil over medium-high heat. Cook 25 to 30 minutes, or until tender; drain. Cool completely, then shred potatoes.

In a medium mixing bowl, combine potatoes and remaining filling ingredients. Place $^1/_2$ cup filling in center of each egg roll skin. Brush edges lightly with water. Fold bottom corners over filling to opposite corners, forming triangles. Press edges to seal.

In a 12-inch nonstick skillet, heat $^1/_4$ cup vegetable oil over medium-high heat. Add turnovers 2 at a time, to skillet. Cook 3 to 4 minutes, or until golden brown, turning once. Drain on paper towel-lined plate. Serve turnovers with salsa. Makes 6 turnovers.

PER TURNOVER: 241 CAL.; 4G PROT.; 13G FAT; 28G CARB.; 4MG CHOL.; 253MG SOD.; 2G FIBER.
OVO-LACTO

'Fried' Green Tomatoes

$^1/_2$ cup yellow cornmeal
$^1/_2$ cup fresh bread crumbs
1 tsp. paprika
$^1/_2$ tsp. salt
$^1/_2$ tsp. black pepper

Dash cayenne pepper (optional)
4 large green tomatoes, horizontally
    cut into $^1/_2$-inch thick slices
1 egg white beaten with 2 Tbs. water
Parmesan cheese (optional)

Preheat oven to 450 degrees. In a shallow dish, combine cornmeal, bread crumbs, paprika, salt, pepper and cayenne, if desired; set aside.

Lightly coat a baking sheet with vegetable cooking spray; set aside. Dip each tomato slice in egg white mixture, then dredge in cornmeal-bread crumb mixture to coat. Place slices in a single layer on prepared baking sheet. Spray tops of slices with vegetable cooking spray.

Bake 30 minutes, or until golden brown. Sprinkle with Parmesan cheese during last 5 minutes of baking if desired. Serve immediately. Makes 6 servings.

PER SERVING: 85 CAL.; 3G PROT.; 1G FAT; 16G CARB.; 0 CHOL.; 271MG SOD.; 2G FIBER.
OVO-LACTO

Veggie-Stuffed Zucchini

Veggie-Stuffed Zucchini

3 medium zucchini (5 oz. each)
1¹/₂ tsp. canola oil
¹/₃ cup chopped onion
2 cloves garlic, minced
1 cup chopped fresh mushrooms
1 medium tomato, chopped (1 cup)

1 Tbs. unseasoned dry bread crumbs
¹/₄ tsp. dried chervil leaves
¹/₈ tsp. pepper
3 Tbs. Parmesan cheese (optional)

Preheat oven to 375 degrees. Cut zucchini in half lengthwise. Scoop out pulp, leaving ¹/₄-inch shells. Coarsely chop pulp. Set shells and pulp aside.

Heat oil over medium heat in a 10-inch nonstick skillet. Stir in onion and garlic. Cook 2 to 3 minutes, or until onion is crisp-tender, stirring occasionally. Add reserved pulp and mushrooms to skillet. Cook 2 to 3 minutes, or until pulp is crisp-tender, stirring frequently. Remove from heat. Stir in tomato, bread crumbs, chervil and pepper.

Spoon mixture evenly into shells. Arrange stuffed zucchini in 11- by 7-inch baking dish. Cover with foil and bake 25 to 30 minutes, or until shells are crisp-tender. Sprinkle with Parmesan cheese. Let stand 5 minutes before serving. Makes 6 servings.

PER SERVING: 38 CAL.; 2G PROT.; 1G FAT; 6G CARB.; 0 CHOL.; 15MG SOD.; 2G FIBER.
VEGAN/LACTO

Herbed Vegetable Bundles

1 lb. broccoli, cut into spears
1 cup julienned carrots
4 green onions, slivered
1 red bell pepper, cut into 8 rings
2 Tbs. white wine

1 tsp. minced fresh cilantro or
     more to taste
1 tsp. minced fresh parsley
4 lemon wedges

Preheat oven to 400 degrees. Tear off 4 large pieces of parchment paper
(about 1 foot square). Fold each square in half and cut a large paper heart.

Open hearts and arrange $^1/_4$ of the broccoli, $^1/_4$ cup carrots, 1 green onion
and 2 rings bell pepper on one half, close to the crease. Drizzle wine over each
pile of vegetables, then top with cilantro and parsley.

Starting at top of heart, hold edges together and fold up a small section
of the rim. Crease and fold up again. Hold down this double-fold as you fold
up adjacent section in the same way. Each fold should slightly overlap the
previous fold to make a secure seal. Place each packet on baking sheet. Bake
15 minutes. Slit open packets and serve with a lemon wedge. Makes 4 servings.

Variations: Experiment with other vegetables, such as asparagus, sliced
squash or sweet potatoes. Instead of white wine, substitute tomato juice,
white grape juice or vegetable broth.

PER SERVING: 63 CAL.; 3G PROT.; <1G FAT; 11G CARB.; 0 CHOL.; 39MG SOD.; 5G FIBER.
VEGAN

Moussaka

2 medium eggplants (about 2 lbs.)
1 tsp. canola oil
2 large onions, chopped
2 cloves garlic, minced
1 medium carrot, diced
1 stalk celery, diced
3 Tbs. tomato paste
1 cup dry red wine (alcoholic or
    non-alcoholic), vegetable
    broth, water or a combination
1 tsp. dried basil
$1/4$ tsp. ground cinnamon, or to taste

1 lb. low-fat tofu
1 cup fat-free cottage cheese
2 Tbs. lemon juice
1 whole egg or $1/4$ cup egg
    substitute (optional)
8 Tbs. Parmesan cheese
Generous pinch nutmeg
$1/2$ tsp. salt (optional)
1 cup whole wheat bread crumbs
$1/2$ cup chopped parsley
3 to 4 firm ripe plum tomatoes,
    thinly sliced

Cut eggplant diagonally into slices no more than $1/3$ inch thick. Spray slices lightly on both sides with vegetable spray; broil in a single layer on both sides 5 minutes, or until lightly browned. Lightly spray a 9- by 11-inch baking dish or oval gratin; set aside.

In a heavy skillet, heat oil. Sauté onion over low heat 2 minutes. Add garlic, carrot and celery; sauté slowly 10 minutes, stirring often, until onion is golden brown. Stir in tomato paste; stir over high heat 1 to 2 minutes to darken or caramelize paste. Add wine, basil and cinnamon. Cover and simmer 2 minutes.

Preheat oven to 375 degrees. In a food processor fitted with a steel blade, combine tofu, cottage cheese, lemon juice, egg or egg substitute, if desired, 4 tablespoons Parmesan, nutmeg and salt if desired. Process until smooth.

Sprinkle a few bread crumbs into baking dish. Add a layer of eggplant slices. Spoon half the vegetable mixture on top of eggplant and spread evenly. Sprinkle mixture with more bread crumbs and 2 tablespoons Parmesan. Repeat layers, using rest of eggplant, vegetable mixture, bread crumbs and cheese. Sprinkle with parsley; add tomato slices in a layer, overlapping to cover. Top with tofu custard, spreading to pan edges. Sprinkle lightly with additional nutmeg; bake 1 hour. Allow to cool completely before serving. Cut into squares to serve. Makes 6 servings.

PER SERVING: 269 CAL.; 15G PROT.; 4G FAT; 34G CARB.; 8MG CHOL.; 485MG SOD.; 5G FIBER.
OVO-LACTO

Whole Wheat Squash Quiche

Whole Wheat Squash Quiche

Crust:
1 cup whole wheat flour
$^1/_2$ tsp. salt
$^1/_3$ cup vegetable shortening
3 to 4 Tbs. cold water
1 acorn squash ($1^1/_4$ lbs.), peeled
    and cut into 1-inch cubes
$^1/_2$ cup water
1 medium zucchini squash, sliced
    (1 cup)

$^1/_2$ cup finely chopped onion
2 Tbs. all-purpose flour
$^1/_4$ tsp. salt (optional)
$^1/_4$ tsp. freshly ground pepper
$^1/_4$ tsp. ground nutmeg
$^1/_3$ cup skim milk
1 cup egg substitute

Preheat oven to 375 degrees. In a large mixing bowl, combine whole wheat flour, salt and shortening. Beat at low speed of electric mixer until particles resemble coarse crumbs.

Sprinkle cold water over flour mixture, 1 tablespoon at a time, mixing with a fork until particles are moistened and cling together. Form dough into a ball. Place ball between two sheets of wax paper and roll into an 11-inch circle. Remove top sheet of wax paper. Turn circle over onto 9-inch pie plate; remove second sheet of wax paper. Flute edges of crust. Prick bottom of crust with fork at 1-inch intervals. Bake 10 minutes. Remove from oven; set crust aside.

In a 2-quart saucepan, combine acorn squash and water. Bring to a boil over medium-high heat. Reduce heat to medium-low. Cover and simmer 10 minutes. Stir in zucchini and onion. Cover and simmer an additional 10 to 13 minutes, or until squash is tender. Drain and set aside.

In a medium mixing bowl, combine all-purpose flour, salt, pepper and nutmeg. Blend in milk. Stir in egg substitute. Add milk mixture to squash mixture. Pour into prepared crust. Bake 30 to 35 minutes, or until quiche is set and knife inserted in center comes out clean. Makes 4 to 6 servings.

PER SERVING: 357 CAL.; 12G PROT.; 19G FAT; 40G CARB.; <1MG CHOL.; 494MG SOD.; 8G FIBER.
OVO-LACTO

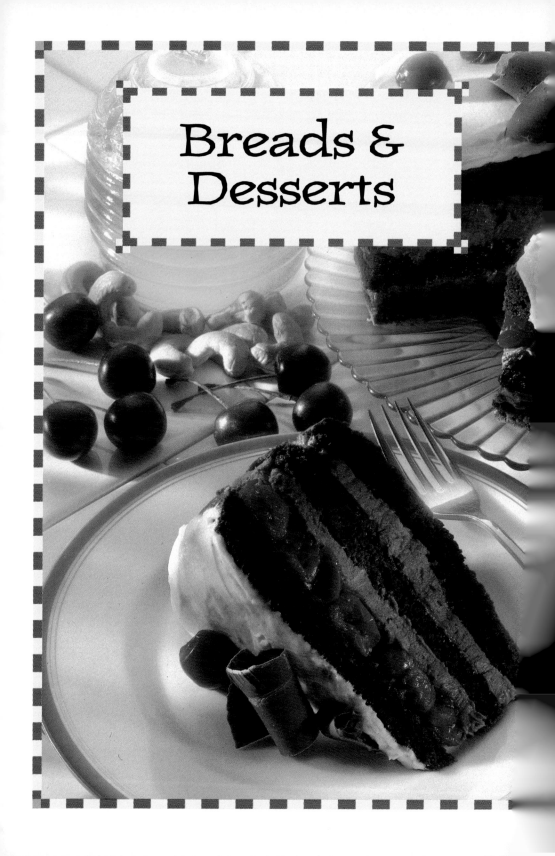

Breads &
Desserts

Black Forest Cake, see page 78

Black Forest Cake

Cake:
1 cup water
1 cup honey
$1/2$ cup applesauce
1 tsp. vanilla
1 tsp. vinegar
2 cups whole wheat pastry flour or
    unbleached white flour
$3/4$ cup cocoa
1 Tbs. baking powder
1 tsp. baking soda

Syrup:
$1/2$ cup water
$1/4$ cup honey

2 thin lemon or orange slices
$1/3$ cup kirsch (cherry liqueur),
    or light or gold rum

Icing:
$3/4$ cup raw cashews
$1/2$ cup water
2 tsp. vanilla
$1/2$ cup honey
10 oz. firm tofu
3 oz. semi-sweet chocolate, melted
16-oz. jar or can pitted cherries,
    drained (not maraschino)

Chocolate curls to garnish (optional)

Cake: Preheat oven to 350 degrees. Combine liquid ingredients in a large bowl; whisk well. Sift dry ingredients together, and whisk into liquid mixture. Pour into a greased and floured 9-inch cake pan. Bake about 35 minutes, or until springy. Cool cake completely; remove from pan. With a serrated knife, cut cake horizontally to make 3 thin layers.

Syrup: Combine water, honey, and lemon or orange slices in a small pan and boil 3 minutes. Let cool, then add kirsch or rum.

Icing: In a blender, combine cashews, water and vanilla. Blend until smooth and creamy. Add honey and tofu; blend again. Set aside 2 cups of mixture for vanilla icing on top and sides of cake. Add melted chocolate and 3 tablespoons syrup to mixture still in blender. Blend again until smooth. Chill both icings before using.

To assemble: Carefully remove two top layers of cake. Brush some syrup onto bottom layer; spread half the chocolate icing on it. Place middle cake layer on top. Brush with more syrup, and spread rest of chocolate icing over it. Put down a layer of cherries, and dot with vanilla icing to help top layer stick. Place top layer on cherries; brush again with syrup. Frost top and sides of cake with vanilla icing, and decorate with cherries and pipe rosettes with a pastry bag, if desired. Garnish with chocolate curls, if desired.

Chill several hours before serving. Cake can be kept covered if not being served until the following day. However, frosting tends to discolor after about 3 days. Makes 12 servings.

PER SERVING: 419 CAL.; 9G PROT.; 9G FAT; 72G CARB.; 1MG CHOL.; 188MG SOD.; 6G FIBER.
VEGAN

Apple and Apricot
Poached Pears

2 Tbs. sugar
1 Tbs. plus 1 tsp. cornstarch
1 1/2 cups unsweetened apple juice
1 tsp. vanilla
1/3 cup chopped dried apricots

2 fresh Bartlett pears, cored and
   cut in half lengthwise
Chopped crystallized ginger
   (optional)

Combine sugar and cornstarch in a 2-quart saucepan. Blend in juice and
vanilla. Stir in apricots. Cook over medium heat 4 to 6 minutes, stirring
frequently, or until mixture is slightly thickened and translucent and begins
to bubble.

Reduce heat to medium-low. Add pear halves. Cook 10 to 18 minutes, or
until pears are tender. Using a slotted spoon, remove pears from poaching
liquid. Serve warm or chilled with poaching liquid. Lightly sprinkle each
serving with ginger. Makes 4 servings.

PER SERVING: 155 CAL.; 1G PROT.; 1G FAT; 39G CARB.; 0 CHOL.; 4MG SOD.; 3G FIBER.
VEGAN

Pumpkin Mousse
with Ginger Cream

Mousse:
16-oz. can pumpkin (about 2 cups)
2 $10^1/2$-oz. packages extra-firm
   silken tofu
$1/3$ cup sugar or maple sugar
   granules
1 Tbs. grated ginger root
$1/2$ tsp. grated nutmeg
1 Tbs. pumpkin pie spice

Cream:
7 oz. extra-firm silken tofu
$2^1/2$ Tbs. fruit-sweetened
   marmalade
1 tsp. grated ginger root
Dash ground cinnamon

Mousse: Combine all mousse ingredients in a food processor or blender. Blend until light and velvety, about 3 minutes. Transfer to a bowl, cover and chill several hours or overnight.

Cream: Purée tofu until creamy. Transfer to a bowl and stir in marmalade and ginger; chill until needed.

To Serve: Serve cold mousse in 8 chilled sorbet or martini glasses. Top each with a dollop of Ginger Cream and a dusting of cinnamon. Makes 8 servings.

Variation: Instead of pumpkin, substitute another variety of winter squash. Steam squash, purée and cook slowly in a nonstick skillet until thick.

PER SERVING: 185 CAL.; 12G PROT.; 7G FAT; 18G CARB.; 0 CHOL.; 16MG SOD.; 2G FIBER.
VEGAN

Ginger Upside-Down Cake

Fruit:
1 Tbs. maple syrup
2 to 3 large ripe peaches or pears

Cake:
4 oz. firm tofu, cubed
1 cup plus 1 Tbs. unsweetened
   apple juice
Grated zest of 1 lemon

$^1/_4$ cup sunflower oil or other light
   vegetable oil
$^1/_3$ cup maple syrup
2 cups sifted whole wheat pastry
   flour
$^1/_2$ tsp. salt
1 tsp. baking soda
1 tsp. ground ginger
$^1/_4$ tsp. ground allspice

Fruit: Lightly grease an 8-inch square glass or ceramic baking pan and drizzle syrup over bottom. Peel and pit or core peaches or pears. Cut lengthwise into $^1/_4$-inch thick slices. Arrange in even rows on bottom of prepared pan.

Cake: Preheat oven to 350 degrees. In a food processor or blender, thoroughly blend tofu and apple juice. Pour into a mixing bowl, then whisk in lemon zest, oil and maple syrup.

Sift together flour, salt, baking soda, ginger and allspice. Gradually add dry ingredients to wet mixture, whisking gently, just until a smooth batter forms. Pour evenly over fruit slices.

Bake 40 minutes, or until tester inserted into center comes out clean. Cool briefly on a rack, then invert onto a large cake plate. Serve warm or at room temperature. Makes 8 servings.

Helpful Hint: To peel peaches, immerse briefly in boiling water and then in cold water; the skins will slip off easily.

PER SERVING: 236 CAL.; 5G PROT.; 8G FAT; 27G CARB.; 0 CHOL.; 242MG SOD.; 4G FIBER.
VEGAN

Indian Pudding

Indian Pudding

$^2/_3$ cup yellow cornmeal
$^1/_4$ tsp. salt
$^1/_2$ tsp. ground ginger
$^1/_4$ tsp. nutmeg

4 cups milk or soymilk
6 Tbs. maple syrup
2 Tbs. hazelnut butter
$^2/_3$ cup raisins or currants

Preheat oven to 275 degrees. Lightly grease a 1½- to 2-quart baking dish.

Sift together cornmeal, salt, ginger and nutmeg. In a saucepan, heat 3 cups milk or soymilk to boiling. Whisk in maple syrup. Gradually add dry mixture, whisking constantly. Reduce heat to low and cook, stirring often, about 10 minutes, until cornmeal mixture is thick and smooth.

Thoroughly whisk in hazelnut butter and stir in raisins or currants. Transfer to prepared baking dish. Pour remaining 1 cup milk or soymilk on top of cornmeal mixture. Bake 2½ hours, or until milk or soymilk is absorbed and top of pudding is well browned. Serve warm. Makes 4 to 6 servings.

PER SERVING: 384 CAL.; 12G PROT.; 9G FAT; 64G CARB.; 10MG CHOL.; 263MG SOD.; 4G FIBER.
LACTO/VEGAN

TIP: Hazelnut butter is available in natural food and specialty stores, but you can make your own. Toast shelled nuts (about twice as much as the amount of nut butter you need) in a 325-degree oven about 10 minutes. Cool nuts briefly, then wrap in a kitchen towel and rub to remove as much of the skins as possible. Blend nuts in a food processor or blender until creamy.

Apricot Bread

Apricot Bread

1 cup all-purpose flour
$^{3}/_{4}$ cup whole wheat flour
$^{1}/_{2}$ cup packed brown sugar
$1^{1}/_{2}$ tsp. baking soda
$^{1}/_{4}$ tsp. ground cardamom
1 cup buttermilk

$^{1}/_{4}$ cup egg substitute or 1 egg,
   beaten
2 Tbs. vegetable oil
$^{1}/_{2}$ cup Grape-Nuts cereal
$^{1}/_{2}$ cup chopped dried apricots

Preheat oven to 350 degrees. Spray an $8^{1}/_{2}$ - b y $4^{1}/_{2}$ -inch loaf pan with vegetable cooking spray and dust lightly with all-purpose flour. Set aside.

Combine flours, sugar, baking soda and cardamom in a large mixing bowl. Add buttermilk, egg or egg substitute, and oil. Beat at low speed of electric mixer just until blended, scraping sides of bowl frequently. Fold in cereal and apricots.

Pour mixture into prepared pan. Bake 45 to 50 minutes, or until tooth-pick inserted in center comes out clean. Let stand 10 minutes. Remove loaf from pan. Cool completely on wire rack before slicing. Makes 16 slices.

PER SLICE: 114 CAL.; 3G PROT.; 2G FAT; 22G CARB.; 1MG CHOL.; 46MG SOD.; 2G FIBER.
OVO-LACTO

Sweet-Tart Cranberry Muffins

1¹/4 cups unbleached white flour
¹/2 tsp. ground cinnamon
¹/2 tsp. ground cardamom
¹/2 tsp. ground nutmeg
1 tsp. baking powder
¹/2 tsp. baking soda
¹/2 tsp. salt
¹/2 cup finely chopped pitted prunes

¹/2 cup rolled oats
³/4 cup buttermilk or soymilk
3 Tbs. canola oil
6 Tbs. maple syrup
¹/2 cup fresh or frozen cranberries
3 egg whites, lightly beaten (or Egg
    Replacer equivalent to 2 eggs)

Preheat oven to 400 degrees. Line a 12-cup muffin tin with muffin papers. (Or lightly oil muffin tin or spray with vegetable spray.)

In a large bowl, sift together flour, cinnamon, cardamom, nutmeg, baking powder, baking soda and salt. Add prunes and oats; toss to coat. In another bowl, whisk together buttermilk or soymilk, oil, syrup and cranberries. In a third bowl, beat egg whites or Egg Replacer to soft peaks; set aside.

Lightly combine dry and wet ingredients, then fold in egg whites or Egg Replacer until just incorporated. Spoon batter into muffin tins, filling ³/4 full. Bake 12 to 15 minutes, or until muffins are light and springy to the touch. Makes 12 muffins.

PER MUFFIN: 140 CAL.; 4G PROT.; 4G FAT; 17G CARB.; 1MG CHOL.; 212MG SOD.; 2G FIBER.
OVO-LACTO/VEGAN

Lemony Teff Seed Muffins

2¹/₂ cups whole wheat pastry flour
¹/₃ cup teff grain
1 tsp. baking powder
1 tsp. baking soda
¹/₂ tsp. cinnamon
1 egg, beaten, or equivalent Egg
    Replacer

³/₄ cup buttermilk
²/₃ cup honey
¹/₄ cup canola or safflower oil
Juice of 1 lemon
1 tsp. grated lemon rind
1 tsp. vanilla extract

Preheat oven to 350 degrees. Combine flour, teff, baking powder, baking soda and cinnamon in a bowl. In a separate bowl, combine egg or Egg Replacer, buttermilk, honey, oil and lemon juice; beat until smooth. Make a well in center of dry ingredients and pour in wet mixture. Add lemon rind and vanilla. Stir vigorously until smooth.

Pour batter into oiled muffin tin or muffin cups and bake 15 to 20 minutes, or until a knife inserted into center tests clean. Makes 12 muffins.

PER MUFFIN: 117 CAL.; 3G PROT.; 5G FAT; 28G CARB.; 14MG CHOL.; 128MG SOD.; 2G FIBER.
OVO-LACTO/ LACTO

Bagels

Bagels

2 cups warm water	1 gallon water
1 1/2 tsp. sugar	5 Tbs. sugar
1 package dry yeast	1 egg white (optional)
1/2 cup gluten flour	Toppings (optional): poppy seeds;
4 to 5 cups all-purpose flour	minced, sautéed onion;
1 tsp. salt	sesame seeds; caraway seeds

In a small bowl, stir together 1/2 cup warm water, 1 1/2 teaspoons sugar and yeast. Let stand 10 minutes, or until foamy. (If mixture does not foam, yeast is not fresh enough or water was too hot or too cold, and dough will not rise properly.)

In a large bowl, combine gluten flour, 2 cups all-purpose flour, salt and remaining 1 1/2 cups warm water. Add yeast mixture and beat with electric mixer on low speed or by hand at least 5 minutes. Add 2 more cups flour; mix until dough turns into a ball.

Turn dough out onto a floured surface and knead by hand until smooth and elastic, adding more flour if necessary, about 5 minutes. Transfer dough to a lightly oiled bowl. Cover with plastic wrap or a damp kitchen towel and place in a warm, draft-free location. Let dough rise until doubled in size, about 1 hour.

Turn dough onto floured surface again and punch down. Knead until smooth and elastic, about 2 minutes. Divide dough into 12 pieces, and shape each piece into a circle. With your thumb, press a hole in middle. Work bagel around thumb to create desired size hole.

After each bagel is formed, place on a lightly floured surface; cover with a dry towel. When all bagels are formed, cover dry towel with a damp towel and let bagels rest until they are 1 1/2 times their original size (not doubled in bulk), about 30 minutes.

Meanwhile, preheat oven to 425 degrees. Prepare a water bath by bringing 1 gallon water and 5 tablespoons sugar to a boil in a large pot. Reduce heat until water is just simmering.

When bagels have risen, transfer to the simmering bath, no more than 3 at a time, with a slotted spoon. Bagels will sink, then rise to surface. (If they don't sink, they rose too much. There's no harm done; they will just be over-sized and less chewy.) Simmer bagels 1 minute, flip and simmer 1 minute more. Remove to a large baking sheet covered with parchment paper or to a lightly greased air-cushioned baking sheet. (Do not use a regular greased baking sheet; bagels will burn and stick.)

Brush bagels with egg white, if desired, for a high-gloss shine. Sprinkle with desired toppings. If not using egg white, dip bagels in desired toppings and place facedown on baking sheet. Bake in center of oven 10 minutes. Remove from oven and turn over. Bagels should be set but not browned. Bake 10 minutes more or until bagels are toasty brown (some ovens may require as much as 30 minutes of baking).

Cool bagels and store in a plastic bag in refrigerator to keep fresh for several days. Freeze any bagels you won't be consuming within a few days. Makes 12 bagels.

PER BAGEL: 159 CAL.; 5G PROT.; <1G FAT; 30G CARB.; 0 CHOL; 192MG SOD.; 1G FIBER.
VEGAN/OVO-LACTO

Onion and Gorgonzola Stuffed Focaccia

1 small red onion, cut into $^1/4$-inch
    slices
1 small Vidalia onion, cut into $^1/4$-
    inch slices
1 tsp. olive oil
1 Tbs. snipped fresh rosemary leaves
2 cloves garlic, minced

Crust:
1 cup warm water (105 to 115 degrees)
$^1/4$-oz. package quick-rise active
    dry yeast
3 cups flour, divided
$^1/4$ cup olive oil
$^1/2$ tsp. sugar
$^1/2$ tsp. salt
$^1/4$ cup plus 2 Tbs. crumbled
    Gorgonzola cheese, divided

Spray a 12-inch round pizza pan or large baking sheet with vegetable cooking spray; set aside.

In a 10-inch nonstick skillet, combine onions and 1 teaspoon oil. Cook over medium heat 5 to 7 minutes, or until onions are crisp-tender, stirring frequently. Add rosemary and garlic. Cook 1 minute, stirring constantly. Remove from heat; set aside.

In a large mixing bowl, combine water and yeast. Stir until yeast is dissolved. Add $2^1/2$ cups flour and remaining crust ingredients. Stir until dough pulls away from side of bowl. Turn dough out onto lightly floured surface. Knead 5 minutes or until smooth, working in remaining $^1/2$ cup flour as necessary to reduce stickiness. Cover with bowl. Let rest 5 minutes. Divide dough in half.

On a lightly floured surface, roll half of the dough into an 11-inch circle and place on prepared pan. Spoon half of onion mixture onto circle, spreading to within 1 inch of edge. Sprinkle with $^1/4$ cup cheese. Roll second half of dough into an 11-inch circle. Fit second circle over filling, pressing edges to seal.

Preheat oven to 375 degrees. Cover focaccia with a cloth. Let rise in warm place 20 to 25 minutes, or until focaccia is doubled in size and impressions remain when dough is pressed with 2 fingers to about $^1/2$-inch depth. Make indentations randomly in dough with fingertips. Top with remaining onion mixture and 2 tablespoons cheese. Bake 25 to 30 minutes, or until golden brown. Serve warm in wedges. Makes 10 servings.

PER SERVING: 206 CAL.; 5G PROT.; 8G FAT; 29G CARB.; 4MG CHOL.; 286 SOD.; 2G FIBER.
LACTO

Onion and Gorgonzola Stuffed Focaccia

Glossary

Anasazi beans: ancestors to pinto beans, they are similar in size and shape, but maroon with white patches. They also have a fuller, sweeter taste and hold their shape well when cooked.

Arrowroot: a starchy, white powder used for thickening that can be substituted for cornstarch measure for measure.

Asafetida: a spice used in many Indian dishes. It imparts the flavor of garlic and onions and is available at Indian grocery stores and some natural food stores.

Balsamic vinegar: a red-brown vinegar made from grapes and aged like wine. It has a robust sweet-sour flavor.

Buckwheat, buckwheat groats: the hulled, crushed seeds of a plant related to rhubarb. Also called kasha.

Bulgur: cracked wheat that has been hulled and parboiled.

Capers: flower buds of a Mediterranean shrub that are picked and used as a condiment. Available in supermarkets in cans and jars.

Cardamom: small, black fragrant seeds of the Indian ginger plant, used as a seasoning or condiment.

Chèvre: ripened cheese made from goat's milk.

Chervil: herb with a sweet, licorice-type flavor, available in leaves and stems.

Cilantro (fresh coriander): a pungent herb that looks like parsley. Popular in Chinese, Mexican and Middle Eastern cuisine.

Couscous: crushed, steamed and dried durum wheat. Popular in Mexican and Middle Eastern dishes.

Cremini mushrooms: brown Italian mushrooms similar in appearance to domestic button mushrooms. Available in specialty stores and some supermarkets.

Crystallized ginger: ginger cooked in sugar syrup and coated in sugar; also called candied ginger.

Cumin: a seed used heavily in Mexican and Middle Eastern cooking.

Egg Replacer: brand name of a powdered, vegan egg substitute. A combination of starches and leavening agents that binds and leavens cooked and baked foods.

Farmer cheese: a hard cheese with a mild taste similar to that of cottage cheese.

Frisé (curly endive): a large, loose-headed member of the chicory family, with its characteristic bitterness; also spelled frisée.

Hummus: Middle Eastern paste or dip, cooked with a base of puréed garbanzo beans.

Infused oil: any oil steeped with herbs, garlic or seasonings. Often homemade, such oils can also be purchased at gourmet shops and some supermarkets.

Japanese pear: a hybrid of pears and apples. Also called Asian pear or apple-pear.

Kirsch: cherry liqueur.

Kudzu: starchy, white powder used for thickening. Made from the root of the kudzu plant.

Lentils: various small disk-shaped beans available in shades of green, brown and red. Available in supermarkets and natural food stores.

Mirin (rice wine): wine made from fermented and aged rice.

Miso: a salty paste made from cooked, aged soybeans and sometimes grains. Thick and spreadable, it is used as a flavoring and a soup base.

Rice vinegar: vinegar made from fermented rice.

Seitan: a chewy, high-protein food made from boiled or baked wheat gluten.

Serrano peppers: narrow green, yellow or red peppers, popular in salsas. Their heat lies somewhere between jalapeños and cayenne peppers.

Shiitake mushrooms: a flavorful mushroom with a brown cap used in traditional Japanese cuisine. Available dried and fresh at supermarkets and natural food stores.

Soymilk: milk made from soaked, ground, strained soybeans. Available in natural food stores and some supermarkets.

Tamari: a naturally brewed soy sauce that contains no sugar.

Teff: a grain native to Ethiopia used for making bread.

Tempeh: a high-protein cultured food made from soybeans and sometimes grains.

Tofu: a white custardlike food made from soybeans and water, ranging from soft to firm. Rarely served alone, it is bland, and takes on the flavor of whatever it is mixed with. Also called bean curd.

Turmeric: a spice belonging to the ginger family, it is yellow with a woody taste.

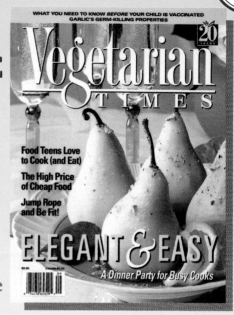

Recipe Index

All recipes are **vegetarian**. They contain no beef, pork, poultry or fish.

Ovo-lacto (O) recipes contain eggs and may also contain dairy products.
Lacto (L) recipes contain dairy products but no eggs.
Vegan (V) recipes contain neither dairy nor eggs (they may contain honey).

Low-fat recipes contain less than 10 grams of fat per serving.

	Page	O/L/V	Low-fat
Appetizers & Snacks			
Asparagus Guacamole	8	L	YES
Caponata	13	L	YES
Cinnamon Chips with Crenshaw Salsa	10	V	YES
Crispy Baked Egg Rolls	12	O	YES
Natural Peanut Butter Fruit Dip	13	L	YES
Seasoned Chips with Lone Star 'Caviar'	15	V	YES
Steamed Vegetable Platter with			
Curried Hummus Dip	9	V	YES
Breads & Desserts			
Apple and Apricot Poached Pears	79	V	YES
Apricot Bread	85	O	YES
Bagels	89	V/O	YES
Black Forest Cake	78	V	YES
Ginger Upside-Down Cake	81	V	YES
Indian Pudding	83	L/V	YES
Lemony Teff Seed Muffins	87	O/L	YES
Onion and Gorgonzola Stuffed Focaccia	90	L	YES
Pumpkin Mousse with Ginger Cream	80	V	YES
Sweet-Tart Cranberry Muffins	86	O/V	YES
Legumes			
Black Bean Quesadillas	40	L/V	NO
Garbanzo Bean and Vegetable Pie	47	O	YES
Lima Bean Succotash	45	L/V	YES
Mediterranean Pot Stickers	44	O	YES
No-Guilt Refried Beans	43	L/V	YES
Pink Beans with Marinated Seitan	41	V	NO
Tri-Bean Bake	43	V	YES
Pasta, Rice & Grains			
Fresh Noodles Lo Mein	53	V	YES
Garlic and Tomato Risotto	50	V/L	YES
Green Rice with Spinach	60	V	YES
Jolof Rice	59	V	YES
Mushroom Stroganoff	51	V	NO
Pasta Pizza	56	L	YES
Polenta Rounds with Sautéed			
Vegetables and Gremolada	63	L/V	YES
Rice and Vegetable Croquettes	61	O	YES
Swedish Wheat Balls	54	O/V	YES
Tabbouleh-Stuffed Avocados	50	V	NO
Vegetable Lasagna	58	O	NO

Recipe Index

Nutritional Information

Calories: The per serving calorie count includes all sources: protein, carbohydrate, fat and alcohol.

Protein: Although protein is most often associated with meat, it is also abundant in many plant foods, particularly in legumes such as beans.

Fat: This measurement includes monounsaturated, polyunsaturated and saturated fats. The percentage of calories from fat is not listed because we believe the percent of fat in a given recipe is less important than the percent of fat eaten in an entire day. To determine that percentage, count the total calories and total fat grams eaten in a day. Multiply grams of fat by 9 (there are 9 calories in a gram of fat) and divide that amount by total calories. Federal guidelines suggest eating no more than 30 percent of calories from fat, but the bulk of research suggests that fat intake must be less than 25 percent of calories to prevent disease and promote health.

Carbohydrates: This measurement includes complex carbohydrate in grains, legumes and vegetables, and simple carbohydrates in fruits and sugars.

Cholesterol: Because cholesterol is found only in animal products, the recipes in this book are extremely low in cholesterol, well below the recommended limit of 300 milligrams (mg.) per day.

Sodium: Sodium intake should not exceed 2,200 to 2,400 milligrams (mg.), which equals about 1 teaspoon of salt.

Fiber (dietary): This measurement indicates the amount of non-absorbable carbohydrate. Fiber is most commonly found in vegetables, fibrous fruits, grains and legumes.